Coming Alongside

Basic Pastoral Care at the Bedside

This basic pastoral care training handbook was written by Jeffrey R Funk, HCMA Executive Director. It is not to be altered in any way—no edits of form or content. Permission for any other use must be obtained in writing from:

Healthcare Chaplains Ministry Association

101 S Kraemer Blvd, Suite 123A
Placentia, California 92870
Phone: (714) 572-3626
Fax: (714) 572-0585
E-mail: info@hcmachaplains.org
Website: www.hcmachaplains.org

God's heart in healthcare since 1939

Table of Contents

Acknowledgements

I have been involved in pastoral care for several decades. I did learn a few things about pastoral ministry at the churches where I have served; however, the in-depth learning about coming alongside has mainly come from my time with HCMA. As a student-Chaplain back in 1991, I received practical insights at USC Medical Center under the tutelage of Chaplain Phil Manly, BCC with HCMA. He is an exemplary Chaplain and has been a faithful mentor and encourager to me throughout my involvement in chaplaincy.

Then, when I became the Executive Director of HCMA, overseeing the training and certification of healthcare Chaplains, I became even more enmeshed in the basics of pastoral care at the bedside and how to impart this understanding to others. I owe the groundwork for this handbook to the initial efforts of Tom Delamater and Timothy Malyon who had the wisdom to see that this chaplaincy care knowledge needed to be composed into a syllabus. They planted the seed for this book that has grown and blossomed out of their original efforts.

I'm grateful to the dedicated and capable HCMA Area Directors and Teaching Chaplains who have given me meaningful feedback on chaplaincy training over these past years. Much, if not most, of the material in this book comes from them and their insights. My name may be on the front cover, but they are the true authors of what it means to be a compassionate pastoral caregiver and how to competently come alongside and comfort those who are crushed in body and spirit.

The HCMA Board of Directors gave me the green light to set aside the necessary time to finalize this book. I'm indebted to their supportiveness of me over these past years. Then there is the HCMA secretary, Anne Miller. She read through the draft and gave me many helpful suggestions for making the content easier to read.

Those of us who teach know that we learn much from our students. About ten years ago Talbot School of Theology gave me the privilege of teaching what is contained in this book to their seminary students. My insights about coming alongside as a pastoral caregiver have been honed by these model students, and by my co-professor, Chaplain Chuck Regehr, BCC with HCMA. He truly has a passion for Christ and a compassion for people and I'm grateful for his practical pastoral insights.

Then there is Joshua, my first-born son, who softened this hard heart and prepared the ground for me to grow into the Chaplain I have become.

Finally, I must acknowledge my beloved wife, Kathryn. She may not be a Chaplain with all the credentials, but I know of no better caregiver who possesses a true pastor's heart because she first of all loves God with her whole being and then His love pours through her into the many lives she touches every day. Besides showing compassion to those on the street in our community, and reaching out with caring notes and phone calls to those in need of encouragement, she was also the primary caregiver for our son Joshua who had major medical problems that ultimately claimed his life at age 24. She is the primary caregiver for our adopted son, Jared, who has significant psychological challenges. In addition, she comforts my soul on a regular basis. She is the consummate example for the lessons in this book about *coming alongside* and I am deeply grateful for her loving and loyal companionship these past 40 years.

Preface

Cure sometimes,
treat often,
comfort always
— Hippocrates (460-370 BC), Greek physician

Blessed be the God and Father of our Lord Jesus Christ,
the Father of mercies and God of all comfort,
who comforts us in all our tribulation,
that we may be able to comfort
those who are in any trouble,
with the comfort with which we ourselves
are comforted by God
— Apostle Paul (2 Corinthians 1:3-4)[1]

This book is not for everyone. Not everyone is called and gifted to come alongside and comfort the hurting. Pastoral care at the bedside is a specialized ministry in a specialized setting. Like the Marines, it's for the few (not necessarily the proud). But for those few (you who are reading this), you know this is what God has called you to do. And this book will help equip you to do what you have been set apart to do.

This basic pastoral care training guide is designed as an essential introduction for those who want to provide pastoral care—comfort—to the hurting. Anyone who is involved in ministering to those who are patients in a hospital or residents in a nursing home or seriously ill folks in hospice will benefit from the information found here, including Chaplains, clergy, lay ministers, and anyone who cares about coming alongside those who are sick and suffering.

By "basic," I mean that what you will find in here will provide some of the essential guidelines that are needed for coming alongside and ministering at the bedside. It will not cover everything you need to know, but it will go over the fundamentals of pastoral care at the bedside. It sets the groundwork upon which you can build your ministry to the sick and suffering, the downhearted and dying.

The word "pastoral" is derived from the image of the shepherd. This rich image is abundant in the Scriptures (over 200 times). No other metaphor has so influenced what it means to do pastoral ministry. For example, the parable of the lost sheep (Luke 15:3-7) is a fitting image for pastoral ministry in the hospital. Many patients in the hospital usually feel cut off from the security of their normal environment. They find their physical bodies suffering and in potential danger. Their emotional selves are often in turmoil as they deal with feeling lonely and scared. Illness can also have a chaotic impact on one's spiritual life, especially if the person is asking God, "Why?" Pastoral caregivers are not focused on the 99 who are secure and at peace, but they reach out with shepherding care to the 1 who feels lost and endangered. This book will help in reaching out to these "lost sheep," in revealing to them the One who leads us beside still waters and restores our souls, in opening their eyes to see the Good Shepherd who walks with us through life's dark and disturbing shadows.

This basic training is about pastoral "care." To the medical team, the patient may be simply the GI bleed in room 114. Our soul care as a shepherd is a meaningful healing remedy to this potential depersonalization of healthcare. We come, not to *treat* them, but to compassionately *care* for them and to remind them of God's shepherding presence and care.

In Ezekiel 34:11-31, God is described as the true Shepherd of Israel who *cares* for the sheep. The care that the medical team provides is different from the care of the pastoral caregiver. Their main focus is on *curing* the body's physical ailments; our main focus is on *caring* for the soul's spiritual needs, on comforting spiritual distress—yet both have a goal of "wellness." The pastoral caregiver, as a caring shepherd, comes alongside to lovingly care for the spiritual needs of the sick and the dying and to remind them of God's loving care for them so they might be whole (well).

By "training," I mean that what is contained in these pages will give basic instructions and guidelines on what is involved in coming alongside within a healthcare setting. It will equip the pastoral caregiver with some basics about how to do ministry at the bedside.

For those interested in an advanced course in clinical pastoral education, it is recommended that you contact Healthcare Chaplains Ministry Association (HCMA) about their Clinical Pastoral Education Program (www.hcmachaplains.org). This specialized chaplaincy training involves four units—1,600 hours—of extensive and intensive chaplaincy training.

Overview of the Book

Here is a brief overview of what you will find in *Coming Alongside* as you read further.

In **Chapter 1**, you will be exposed to the biblical foundation for pastoral care: love and compassion. For some of you, this discussion may get a bit "heavy" and you may get discouraged from reading further. If you want, skip to the chapters that are of interest to you and then come back to this chapter later. It is placed first because it does set forth the primary groundwork for who we are and what we do as pastoral caregivers.

Chapter 2 gives you some very practical guidelines for what to do and what to avoid in coming alongside the hurting. Even those who have some experience doing visitation will find some helpful principles here.

A significant part of pastoral care is about listening to people tell their stories. **Chapter 3** presents some useful insights into giving your full attention to what people have to say, which will help you be a better comforter as you come alongside them.

Chapter 4 discusses our role as a pastoral caregiver—what it is and isn't. You will probably find some aspect of yourself within these pages and gain understanding about being an ambassador, neighbor, and comforter as you come alongside the sick and suffering.

When you start visiting sick folks, some of them are going to die. How will you respond? **Chapter 5** will give you a basic understanding of death and dying and help you to be more comfortable coming alongside the dying and their family during this often difficult journey.

Almost everyone you visit will have some kind of grief issue: they will have moved to a new home, been divorced, had a friendship end, had a job change, lost an ability or function, had a child move out of the home, lost health, lost income, lost hope, and the list goes on and on. All of these losses in life have a grief reaction to them. **Chapter 6** will help you understand this grief reaction and know how to come alongside these hurting people and be with them in a healing way.

In **Chapter 8**, you will come face-to-face with the need for setting boundaries in your ministry in order to protect yourself and those to whom you minister. Don't skip this chapter! Some have ignored the "No Trespassing" signs in their life and ministry and it has had devastating consequences for both their personal lives and the lives of others in connection with them.

I had a friend who was involved in a very successful ministry, but he let the stresses build up to the point that he couldn't take it anymore, so he dropped out. **Chapter 9** is a practical discussion about how to avoid burning out from your giving out of the Gospel. This chapter will encourage you to take care of yourself as you come alongside people in crisis.

You will find **Questions for Review** at the end of each chapter to help you recall major points in each chapter before moving on to the next. They can also be used in a training program for helping to stimulate meaningful dialogue as you learn what's involved in *Coming Alongside*.

Some **Questions for Reflection** are also given at the end of each chapter. It is hoped that these will stimulate insightful thoughts and feelings that will challenge you to go deeper in your understanding and application of the subject.

A bibliography is given at the end of each chapter under the heading **Chapter Resources**. This is not intended to be exhaustive in its content, nor does it contain all of the latest resources. I do not endorse all of the ideas expressed in all of the resources listed. Some of the sources are given simply to expose us to a variety of viewpoints on the subject. It is expected that even in places of disagreement we will reflect upon and think critically regarding our own views rather than simply dismissing views that may run counter to our own.

Coming Alongside

The night before His crucifixion, Jesus said to His disciples, "You are those who have *stood by* Me in My trials" (Luke 22:28, NASB, emphasis added). The body of Christ has an important role to play in "standing by"—*Coming Alongside*—those going through trials in their lives. Somehow many have come to think that only Pastors and Elders can effectively visit the sick. But, as Katie Maxwell put it, "Instead of being the 'players,' the clergy should instead be the 'coaches' for the visiting team."[2] This handbook is designed to help the church leadership coach the equipping of pastoral caregivers. And when the members of this pastoral care team are commissioned before the congregation during a worship service, all members will understand that these folks may be the ones to come visit them, not only the clergy.

Each church needs to establish a pastoral care training program for those who feel called to this type of ministry. This visiting team needs to be willing to commit to training and coaching. Such training will include learning the principles of pastoral care presented in *Coming Alongside*. It will involve meaningful discussions about pastoral care. It will include peer review of visits. This training can be done with a recommended schedule of 10 sessions (one for each of the chapters plus an extra for introduction or conclusion) that are 2-3 hours each: one hour for lecture and discussion, and at least one hour for peer review. With a regular time to learn the basic information, to share about the tough visits, to gain new insights and learn from one another, the visiting team will be better equipped to come alongside the hurting within and without the church body.

For specific information about how to supervise a training program and do peer review of verbatim reports, please contact HCMA at info@hcmachaplains.org, or call us at (714) 572-3626.

Visiting the sick is a high calling to bear one another's burdens. God calls us to comfort those going through trials (2 Corinthians 1:3-7). May going through this basic information help you to be and do all God has called you to be and do as you come alongside those in need of comforting care.

Jeffrey R Funk, MDiv, BCC

1

Biblical Foundation for Pastoral Care: Love and Compassion[1]

Love never asks how little can I do;
. . . love always asks how much.
Love does not merely go the measured mile;
love travels to the uttermost.
Love never haggles, never bargains,
with "nicely calculated less or more."
— George H. Morrison (1866-1928),
Pastor in Glasgow, Scotland

One of the religion scholars. . .put in his question:
"Which is most important of all the commandments?"
Jesus said, "The first in importance is,
'Listen, Israel: The Lord your God is one;
so love the Lord God with all your passion
and prayer and intelligence and energy.'
And here is the second:
'Love others as well as you love yourself.'
There is no other commandment that ranks with these."
— Jesus (Mark 12:28-31, The Message)

A s you begin this basic pastoral care training, here are some important questions to consider and answer before coming alongside people. What is one of the most important principles in our life as a Christian? What is the biblical foundation for our ministry at the bedside?

As a beginning point, consider the question Jesus was asked by a scribe: "Which is the first commandment of all?" (Mark 12:28) Jesus answered the scribe and declared that the number one priority in our life as a Christian is to love God with our whole being: with all our heart, soul, mind and strength (Mark 12:30).

Then Jesus added a second, equally important, priority for our lives: we are to love our neighbor as ourselves (Mark 12:31).

Jesus concluded by saying there is no commandment greater than these two (Mark 12:31). Notice He said no commandment (singular rather than plural) is greater than these. He didn't see loving God as a separate or more important duty from loving one's neighbor.

The Dalai Lama once said, "Love and compassion are necessities, not luxuries. Without them humanity cannot survive." Though his viewpoint is accurate, we will probably prefer to base our pastoral care principles on the Word of God rather than Tibetan Buddhism. However, his statement is another example of how important this issue is and the fact that its truth is upheld even by those who do not know the Chief Shepherd, the Giver of truth and the One who is Truth (John 14:6).

The bottom line for who we are and what we do as a Christian is LOVE. The same is true for who we are and what we do as a pastoral caregiver at the bedside. Love and compassion are at the foundation of Christianity in general and pastoral care in particular.[2]

So let's look at love and compassion—the foundation for pastoral care—as they are developed in the Bible.

Old Testament Principles

In the Beginning. . .

A good place to start is in the book of Genesis, beginning with Adam and Eve in the Garden of Eden. We have all heard the story: God created Adam and Eve and provided everything they needed and then they disobeyed God—they sinned. But because of His love for them, God did not abandon them in their fallen condition. He came to them and His first action, after creating the universe and developing a relationship with Adam and Eve, was to show love for them by providing a covering for the shame of their sin: He shed the blood of an animal in order to clothe them (Genesis 3:21; cf. 2:25). By doing so, God showed, among other things, that love was at the foundation of who He is and what He does. He also inferred the sacrifice of a life for the guilt of their sin (cf. 4:4-5).

As we watch things unfold in Genesis, we see humanity continue to have a bent toward sinfulness. According to Genesis 6:5, "Then the LORD saw that the wickedness of man was great in the earth, and that every intent of the thoughts of his heart was only evil continually."

God was grieved by the evil thoughts and activity of mankind, and purposed to wipe them out, but He showed love toward Noah and his family by providing a way of escape in the Ark. And when the flood was over, He put a rainbow in the sky as a sign of His covenant of loyal love to His creation. That covenant is found in Genesis 9.

But only two chapters later we see the people prideful and pursuing vain glory in an endeavor that was opposed to God's command to fill the earth. This action implies purposeful spiritual distance from God on their part. So God created linguistic chaos in order to disperse them. Commenting on this, Arthur Glasser wrote: "The linguistic diversification at Babel is presented as God's merciful way to avoid destroying the whole human race determined to rebel against Him."[3] In other words, this was another act of love by God toward a rebellious people.

Now God narrows His plan to restore relationship with His people. He chooses to deal with one extended family for the purpose of providing a blessing (redemption) for all the people on earth. God's plan was that through Abraham (Israel) all nations would see and experience God's *hesed*.[4]

HESED

The Hebrew word *hesed* is used 240 times in the Old Testament. And as we look through Scripture, we will see that *hesed* rests at the center of the Lord's revelation of His attitude toward His people. This is especially true in the context of God's covenant with people. He is the God of *hesed*, or "covenant love."

In the Bible it is often translated "mercy" (KJV), steadfast love (RSV), or "lovingkindness" (NASB). Another good expression of the meaning of the word, and the one I like to use, is "loyal love."

In reference to human activity, *hesed* signifies the type of love and duty toward God by which the people of God live in obedience to His ways: loving God and loving neighbors. In reference to divine activity, *hesed* is often used in the context of covenant. *Hesed* is loyal love (fidelity) to a covenant relationship.

Hesed always involves persons, never inanimate objects. It is requested of or done for another where relationship usually has already been established (like in a covenant). *Hesed* is a specific action. It involves *doing* mercy, *showing* lovingkindness, *keeping* loyal love.

From a secular viewpoint, *hesed* is seen in personal and political relationships. Examples of personal *hesed* relationships are when Abraham had Sarah call him her brother, saying "This is your kindness. . ." (Genesis 20:13). Another example is when Abraham's servant, while making the deal with Laban for Rebekah as Isaac's wife, said, "Now if you will deal kindly and truly with my master. . ." (Genesis 24:49). When Jacob was asking Joseph to promise not to bury him in Egypt, he said, "Deal kindly and truly with me." (Genesis 47:29). Boaz said to Ruth, ". . .you have shown more kindness. . ." in referring to her actions toward him (Ruth 3:10). The Lord, in speaking of Israel through the example of Hosea and Gomer, says, ". . .I will have <u>mercy</u> on her who had not obtained <u>mercy</u>. . ." (Hosea 2:23).

Examples of political *hesed* relationships are when Joseph asked the Pharaoh's cup-bearer to "show <u>kindness</u>" to him by remembering his situation when he got out of prison (Genesis 40:14). The king of Syria, Ben-Hadad, had fled from the Israelites after 100,000 of his soldiers had been killed. While hiding, his servants said to him, ". . .we have heard that the kings of the house of Israel are <u>merciful</u> kings. . .perhaps [Ahab] will spare your life." After dressing in sackcloth they came out and "were watching closely to see whether any sign of <u>mercy</u> would come from him [king Ahab]" (1 Kings 20:31, 33). David chose to "show <u>kindness</u> to Hanun the son of Nahash, as his father showed <u>kindness</u> to me." In the relationship between David and Jonathan we see both personal and political *hesed*. We are told that Jonathan loved David as his own soul. David asked Jonathan to deal <u>kindly</u> with him concerning the situation with Saul and Jonathan asked David to show him the <u>kindness</u> of the Lord. This loyal love for one another was confirmed by making a covenant together (1 Samuel 18:1, 3; 20:8, 14-15, 17). David later showed <u>kindness</u> toward Mephibosheth because of that covenant (2 Samuel 9:1, 3, 7).

There are four common features of *hesed*: First, the help is vital because the person in need cannot help himself and the situation will get worse if help is not received. Second, the circumstances dictate that one person is uniquely able to provide the needed assistance. Third, the help is freely given. It is a *willing* decision. Fourth, the one in need has no control over the decision of the person who is in a position to help.

Hesed became the central term in expressing the relationship between God and Israel. According to Dr. Peggy Wobbema,

The duty of mutual service, utilizing loving kindness, was expected on both sides for the covenant to be maintained. As a result of this, Israel held to a strong conviction that God's kindness and readiness to help them was something that could be expected in view of His established covenant relationship with them.[5]

The following Scripture verses will give us some further insights into the meaning of *hesed*.

In the Song of Moses, he proclaims: "You in Your <u>mercy</u> have led forth the people whom You have redeemed; You have guided them in Your strength to Your holy habitation" (Exodus 15:13). Further along in Exodus, we read:

The Lord Himself proclaimed, as He passed before Moses: The Lord, The Lord God, <u>merciful</u> and gracious, longsuffering, and abounding in goodness and truth, keeping <u>mercy</u> for thousands, forgiving iniquity and transgressions and sin. . . (Exodus 34:6-7).

After the spies returned and two said go and ten said no, Moses declared before the whole congregation:

The Lord is longsuffering and abundant in <u>mercy</u>, forgiving iniquity and transgression. . . . Pardon the iniquity of this people, I pray, according to the greatness of Your <u>mercy</u>, just as You have forgiven this people, from Egypt even until now (Numbers 14:18-19).

Many years later[6] the Psalmist recognized God's amazing goodness and grace—His *hesed*—endures forever:

Oh, give thanks to the Lord, for He is good! For His <u>mercy</u> endures forever. Let Israel now say, "His <u>mercy</u> endures forever." Let the house of Aaron now say, "His <u>mercy</u> endures forever." Let those who fear the Lord now say, "His <u>mercy</u> endures forever" (Psalm 118: 1-4).

Likewise, in another post-exilic Psalm, the Psalmist proclaimed that no matter what is going on in our lives, God is working out a plan according to His *hesed*:

Oh, give thanks to the Lord, for He is good! For His <u>mercy</u> endures forever. . .Whoever is wise will observe

20

these things, and they will understand the <u>lovingkindness</u> of the LORD (Psalm 107:1, 43).

Here is a Psalm of David where he has been comparing God's *hesed* to the sea, sky, and mountains (Psalm 36:5-6) and then he proclaims:

How precious is Your <u>lovingkindness</u>, O God! Therefore the children of men put their trust under the shadow of Your wings. They are abundantly satisfied with the fullness of Your house, and You give them drink from the river of Your pleasures. For with You is the fountain of life; in Your light we see light. Oh, continue your <u>lovingkindness</u> to those who know You, and Your righteousness to the upright in heart (Psalm 36:7-10).

RAHAM

There is another Hebrew word that is foundational to pastoral care and also involves love: the word *raham*. It is found 133 times in the Old Testament. Of the 47 uses of the verb, 35 speak of God's love for human beings. It is often translated "to love deeply," "to have mercy," and "to be compassionate."

Webster's Dictionary had this meaningful definition for the word "compassion": *the act or capacity for sharing in the painful feelings of another*. That's appropriate since the English word comes from the Latin *com + pati*, which literally means "to suffer with."

Webster's Dictionary also had this discerning definition for "mercy" (the English word sometimes translated for *raham*): *compassion expressed toward an offender resulting in blessing that is an act of divine favor and compassionate treatment of those who are suffering*.

Some biblical examples of its usage include comparing a father's love for his children with God's love for those who fear Him: "As a father <u>pities</u> his children, so the Lord <u>pities</u> those who fear Him" (Psalm 103:13). After describing the extreme afflictions he has experienced (Lamentations 3:1-18), Jeremiah still had hope because he could count on God's *raham* to always be available to him: ". . .through the Lord's mercies (*hesed*) we are not consumed, because His <u>compassions</u> fail not. They are new every morning. . ." (Lamentations 3:18-23). In describing the kings of Israel who "did evil in the sight of the Lord," as well as all the leaders and priests and the people who transgressed more and more, the Bible says: "And the Lord God of their fathers sent warnings to them by His messengers, rising up early and sending them, because He had <u>compassion</u> on His people and on His dwelling place" (2 Chronicles 36:15).

Raham clearly indicates the depth of the relationship God has with His people, but it also reflects His sovereign choice to love these people unconditionally: "I will have <u>compassion</u> on whom I will have <u>compassion</u>" (Exodus 33:19; cf. Romans 9:15).

God's forgiveness (which involves both His *hesed* and *raham*) for people who really deserve judgment is expressed in Deuteronomy 13:17,

> *So none of the accursed things shall remain in your hand, that the Lord may turn from the fierceness of His anger and show you mercy (hesed), have <u>compassion</u> on you and multiply you, just as He swore to your fathers.*

God's loyal love and compassion in persevering with His disobedient people is shown in 2 Kings 13:23,

> *But the Lord was gracious to them, had <u>compassion</u> on them, and regarded them, because of His covenant with Abraham, Isaac, and Jacob, and would not yet destroy them or cast them from His presence.*

God's *raham* toward His people resulted in the Israelites understanding that they were to display similar compassionate actions towards their brethren. For example, "He has shown you, O man, what is good; and what does the Lord require of you but to do justly, to love <u>mercy</u>, and to walk humbly with your God?" (Micah 6:8). This is consistent with what Isaiah had instructed: "Learn to do good; seek justice, rebuke the oppressor; defend the fatherless, plead for the widow" (Isaiah 1:17). These actions are all examples of compassion. Proverbs instructs: "He who has <u>pity</u> on the poor lends to the Lord, and He will pay back what he has given" (Proverbs 19:17).

This compassion was not to be reserved only for those who are lovable and similar to us in culture and beliefs. It was also to be displayed toward the foreigners who were different than us. While explaining the rules and regulations for the Israelites, Moses said, "You shall neither mistreat a stranger nor oppress him, for you were strangers in the land of Egypt" (Exodus 22:21). Similarly, "Also you shall not oppress a stranger, for you know the heart of a stranger, because you were strangers in the land of Egypt" (Exodus 23:9). And God is the ultimate example of this kind of compassion: "He administers justice for the fatherless and the widow, and loves the stranger, giving him food and clothing" (Deuteronomy 10:18).

Human *raham* was experienced and expected as a duty in the context of family relationships. But *raham* was to be extended not only to our neighbor, but also to strangers, and especially those who were in need or oppressed. A lack of compassion was characteristic of those who were considered immoral. For example, in Proverbs it says: "The soul of the wicked desires evil; his neighbor finds no favor in his eyes" (Proverbs 21:10).

Furthermore, regarding strangers, widows and orphans, we are to avoid doing things that will "afflict" them:

> *You shall neither mistreat a stranger nor oppress him, for you were strangers in the land of Egypt. You shall not afflict any widow or fatherless child. If you afflict them in any way, and they cry at all to Me, I will surely hear their cry* (Exodus 22:21-23).

I think the opposite of afflicting them is showing them love and compassion. And God is the example of such compassion that we, as His followers, should be imitating. Look at Psalm 72:12-14, which says:

*For He will deliver the needy when he cries, the poor
also, and him who has no helper. He will spare the poor
and needy, and will save the souls of the needy. He will
redeem their life from oppression and violence; and precious shall their blood be in His sight.*

Job, who was considered by God as one who was blameless
and upright, understood this principle. He was aware that there
would be a day when he would be required to give an account to
God for his treatment of others. He said,

*"If I have despised the cause of my male or female ser-
vant when they complained against me, what then shall
I do when God rises up? When He punishes, how shall I
answer Him? Did not He who made me in the womb make
them? Did not the same One fashion us in the womb? If
I have kept the poor from their desire, or caused the eyes
of the widow to fail, or eaten my morsel by myself, so that
the fatherless could not eat of it . . . if I have seen anyone
perish for lack of clothing, or any poor man without covering; if his heart has not blessed me, and if he was not
warmed with the fleece of my sheep; if I have raised my
hand against the fatherless, when I saw I had help in the
gate; then let my arm fall from my shoulder, let my arm be
torn from the socket. . .If I have rejoiced at the destruction
of him who hated me, or lifted myself up when evil found
him (indeed I have not allowed my mouth to sin by asking
a curse on his soul); if the men of my tent have not said,
'who is there that has not been satisfied with his meat?'
(But no sojourner had to lodge in the street, for I have
opened my doors to the traveler). . ."* (Job 31:13-32).

New Testament Principles

The love and compassion of God in the Old Testament is
known in and through Jesus Christ in the New Testament. In Christ
all the fullness of God dwelled (Colossians 2:9), and love and
compassion were clearly seen in how Jesus treated people from

every walk of life, especially those who were needy or suffering. Christ's teaching and example would challenge the parameters of love and compassion normally expressed by the Jews for their friends and neighbors, even to the point of loving one's enemies. Jesus taught the multitudes,

> *You have heard that it was said, 'You shall love your neighbor and hate your enemy.' But I say to you, love your enemies, bless those who curse you, do good to those who hate you, and pray for those who spitefully use you and persecute you. . .* (Matthew 5:43-48).

In the New Testament there is a classic story that gives a dynamic example of what it means to have love and compassion for people. The familiar passage is found in Luke 10:25-37. The parable of the Good Samaritan is a classic teaching story similar to any teaching tradition: the teacher tells the story and then turns the question beyond the boundaries of the questioner. Before getting into the details of the story, there is some background information to consider.

There are two basic premises when thinking about reaching out to those in need within the Jewish culture. The first premise is that sharing goods with the needy was anchored in social relationships. To share with someone in need without expecting anything in return was to treat others as if they were family.

In Luke 18:18-23, Jesus was asked, "What shall I do to inherit eternal life?" Jesus reminded him of the commandments to not commit adultery or murder or theft or lying and to honor his parents. The guy basically said, "No problem." Jesus responded by adding one more requirement: "Go sell all that you have and distribute it to the poor. . .and come follow Me." But the guy wasn't willing to show compassion for the needy, which revealed the true character of his heart.

The second premise concerns the patron-client relationship. First century Judaism was ordered by boundaries with specific rules and regulations regarding how Jews should treat other people, including Gentiles and Samaritans. They had guidelines for how priests should relate to others. They had policies for how men were to treat women. And the list goes on and on. Jesus greatly stretched these boundaries when He said,

> *Give to everyone who asks of you. And from him who takes away your goods do not ask for them back. And just as you want men to do to you, you also do to them likewise. . .But love your enemies, do good, and lend, hoping for nothing in return. . .be merciful, just as your Father also is merciful* (Luke 6:30-36).

Let's now look at the two key Greek words used in the New Testament for love and compassion.

LOVE

The first Greek word is *agapē* (love). It appears about 320 times in the New Testament and the word is found in every New Testament Book. *Agapē* love "has its basis in preciousness, a love called out of one's heart by an awakened sense of value in the object loved that causes one to prize it. . . . It is a love that recognizes the worthiness of the object loved."[7] For example, it occurs in John 3:16 where God's love demonstrated for sinners at Calvary springs from His heart in response to the precious value He places on every human soul. In the Incarnation and Crucifixion, Christ is the ultimate expression of God's love for all of humanity.

Agapē is not simply a loving feeling, but it is a love of self-sacrifice and an active commitment of choice. We purpose to do loving deeds for others as part of a Christian lifestyle that shows we are Christ followers. As Paul said, we are to "walk [live] in love, as Christ also has loved us and given Himself for us, an offering and a sacrifice to God for a sweet-smelling aroma" (Ephesians 5:2). This transforming love of God within us compels us to have a practical concern for others that leads us to reach out and meet the needs of others. As the Apostle John said,

> *By this we know love, because He laid down His life for us. And we also ought to lay down our lives for the brethren. But whoever has the world's goods, and sees*

his brother in need, and shuts up his heart from him, how does the love of God abide in him? My little children, let us not love in word or in tongue, but in deed and in truth (1 John 3:16-18).

COMPASSION

The second Greek word is *splanchnizomai* (compassion). It is tenderness and affection that comes from deep within us. "The word originally indicated the inner parts of the body and came to suggest the seat of the emotions—particularly emotions of pity, compassion, and love."[8] This compassion is always more than gut feelings. It takes action to help those whose needs have moved the person. It is willful affection that is moved to help those in need. And this compassionate action of one person has the potential of changing the life of another person. This is because the person moved to loving action gets involved enough in the needy person's life so that the person is set on a fresh, new course in life.

This brings us back to the original mandate to love God and our neighbor. God's claim on us reaches to every area of our existence: our heart (emotional resources), our soul (that inner person, which gives us our identity), our mind (understanding and intellectual capacities), and our strength (energy, might, resolve, physical resources).

When Jesus answered the lawyer's question with the Good Samaritan story, He did not distinguish between separate areas of human life, but showed complimentary aspects of human responsibility. The message is crystal clear: We cannot claim to have love for God and yet not love those whom God loves. The converse is also true: We cannot love our neighbor with a truly divine quality of love unless we also love God deeply (see 1 John 3:16-17; 4:20-21).

In the story it says the Samaritan "took pity" (had compassion) on the abused man. Love and compassion for needy people should prompt a Christian to have a commitment to protect and provide for those people. The compassion felt by the Samaritan prompted him to loving action—he saw the need and took action to do something about meeting the need.

The Principle of Selflessness

Selflessness involves seeing beyond ourselves and seeing clearly the needs of others. Love and compassion are not self-seeking (1 Corinthians 13:5), but they seek the good of others in need (1 Corinthians 10:24). They are willing to sacrifice self and personal needs (Ephesians 5:1-2), even to the point of suffering alongside the hurting (1 Peter 2:20-21). Love and compassion are selfless acts of mercy toward the needy—even to the extent of taking time to pray for our adversaries (Matthew 5:44; Luke 6:35-36).

The Principle of Dignity and Impartiality

The Samaritan is depicted as the hero of the story. He is given attributes of kindness, compassion, self-sacrifice, and caring for the suffering.

The wounded man is not characterized by anything other than his needy condition. He is left with nothing to identify who he is except his desperate need. He is stripped of any identity or dignity. However, the compassion showed to him by the Samaritan helped restore his dignity.

This is not much different than the people we will meet in the hospital or nursing home or in hospice care while making visits. Their only identity is being a sick or lonely person in need of spiritual and emotional support. Having been placed in a skimpy hospital gown, and often treated as nothing more than their illness, they lack dignity. Even so, the pastoral caregiver's loving and compassionate care can reignite a sense of value and dignity in a patient's or resident's personhood.

It is fundamental to view sick and suffering people as being created in the image of God. Each person is worthy of love, respect and care, even those with disgusting diseases and loathsome lifestyles. The Old Testament is very clear about this principle: God shows no partiality for anyone. Consider the following Scripture verses:

Deuteronomy 10:17 declares: *"For the L*ORD *your God is God of gods and Lord of lords, the great God, mighty and awesome, who shows no partiality nor takes a bribe."*

In 1 Samuel 16:7, when Samuel was selecting a new king for Israel, God told him:

*"Do not look at his appearance or at his physical stature, because I have refused him. For the L*ORD *does not see as man sees; for man looks at the outward appearance, but the L*ORD *looks at the heart."*

Job 34:19 makes it very clear that God *"is not partial to princes, nor does He regard the rich more than the poor, for they are all the work of His hands."*

And the New Testament is consistent with the Old in this perspective. After the experience with Cornelius in Caesarea, Peter said: *"In truth I perceive that God shows no partiality"* (Acts 10:34).

Paul proclaimed:

But from those who seemed to be something—whatever they were, it makes no difference to me; God shows personal favoritism to no man—for those who seemed to be something added nothing to me (Galatians 2:6).

James said:

If you really fulfill the royal law according to the Scripture, 'You shall love your neighbor as yourself,' you do well; but if you show partiality, you commit sin, and are convicted by the law as transgressors (James 2:8-9).

James also states that to show partiality is tantamount to being a judge characterized by evil thoughts (2:4).

The poor, disenfranchised and marginalized in society are precious to God, and therefore they should be precious to us as well. Moses declared that God "administers justice for the fatherless and the widow, and loves the stranger, giving him food and clothing" (Deuteronomy 10:18). The Psalmist said, "The Lord watches over the strangers; He relieves the fatherless and widow; but the way of the wicked He turns upside down" (Psalm 146:9). Isaiah affirmed:

> *The Spirit of the LORD God is upon Me, because the LORD has anointed Me to preach good tidings to the poor; He has sent Me to heal the brokenhearted, to proclaim liberty to the captives, and the opening of the prison to those who are bound* (Isaiah 61:1; compare Luke 4:18 where Jesus applied this passage to Himself as Messiah).

In clarifying His ministry to John the Baptist, Jesus said, ". . .the blind see, the lame walk, the lepers are cleansed, the deaf hear, the dead are raised, the poor have the gospel preached to them" (Luke 7:22). James stated: "Pure and undefiled religion before God and the Father is this: to visit orphans and widows in their trouble. . ." (James 1:27).

Jesus made no distinction between classes of people in Matthew 25. The main issue was people who had needs that were either ignored by some or were met by others who cared enough to come alongside and get involved by feeding the hungry, giving water to the thirsty, by taking in strangers, by clothing the naked, and by visiting the sick and those in prison. The One who holds the fate of all humankind in His hands cares about those who have basic needs.

The ministry of Jesus touched the lives of those who were disenfranchised, hurting and suffering. And His expectation of the people of God is no less!

The Principle of Continuous Care

I don't know what "pastoral presence" means to most people. For some, it simply means being fully with those who are hurting. But the story of the Good Samaritan goes beyond occasional presence and emphasizes the principle of a willingness to *remain* involved with suffering people *through* each stage of difficulty.

He wasn't temporarily taking part in the person's pain. He was committed to coming alongside in ongoing care.

The Samaritan initially attended to the wounded man's immediate needs: he comforted the hurting person and bandaged his injuries as best he could. Then he helped transport him to the nearest city. And when he got there he provided lodging and promised to return to check up on him. The Samaritan demonstrated pastoral care that was willing to get involved for the long-term rather than only the short-term.

Professor Ian Gentles made this comment:

> *One of the greatest gifts you and I can give to another human being is the gift of an attentive, listening mind, coupled with a sincere attempt to understand his or her needs. Your genuine presence and care itself will demonstrate the love of God, as you share for brief periods another's pilgrimage through the valley of the shadow. You will be a sacrament of the very presence of the Good Shepherd Himself.*[9]

In Conclusion

At the end of the story, Jesus said, *"Go and do likewise!"* This is the challenge to every pastoral caregiver who wants to come alongside people who are suffering: to go and demonstrate the love and compassion of God to hurting and needy people. This love and compassion is the very heart, the foundation, of our pastoral care ministry. As a Christian pastoral caregiver, we are to value acts of mercy over personal productivity. But it's not easy to do this. As Henri Nouwen points out:

> *Let us not underestimate how hard it is to be compassionate. Compassion is hard because it requires the inner disposition to go with others to the place where they are weak, vulnerable, lonely, and broken. But this is not our spontaneous response to suffering. What we desire most is to do away with suffering by fleeing from it or finding a quick cure for it. As busy, active, relevant ministers, we*

31

want to earn our bread by making a real contribution. This means first and foremost doing something to show that our presence makes a difference.[10]

This love and compassion is often accomplished simply by coming alongside to offer our quiet pastoral presence to the sick and suffering. May God's love and compassion flow freely from our hearts and actions as we come alongside people in need.

Questions for Review

1. How would you explain to someone what *hesed* means?
2. How do you explain what *raham* means?
3. What are the New Testament equivalents to *hesed* and *raham*, and how do you, in your own words, give examples of what they mean?
4. According to the Good Samaritan story, what are you supposed to be doing in response to those in need?

Questions for Reflection

1. Spend several minutes in Bible study, reflection and prayer on how God's love and compassion has touched your life personally. (This is outside of your salvation experience.) How will these experiences impact your pastoral care ministry? Record your insights in a journal and share them with a confidant and/or the training team.
2. Do a word study on God's character (especially His *hesed* and *raham*) as revealed in the Psalms. How will this knowledge impact your personal life as well as the pastoral care you provide? Record your insights and share them with a confidant and/or the training team.
3. Since love and compassion are foundational qualities for a pastoral care ministry, write a one-page "defense" for why, in light of these necessary qualities, you should

be involved in pastoral care at the bedside. Discuss your insights with another person involved in pastoral care.

Chapter Resources

Arnold, William V. *Introduction to Pastoral Care*. Philadelphia: Westminster, 1982.

Clinton, Timothy, and George Ohlschlager, eds. *Competent Christian Counseling*. Colorado Springs, CO: WaterBrook, 2002.

Collins, Gary R. *The Biblical Basis of Christian Counseling for People Helpers*. Colorado Springs, CO: NavPress, 1993.

Fowler, James W. *Faith Development and Pastoral Care*. Minneapolis: Fortress, 1987.

Gerkin, Charles V. *An Introduction to Pastoral Care*. Nashville: Abingdon, 1997.

Hurding, Roger F. *The Tree of Healing: Psychological & Biblical Foundations for Counseling and Pastoral Care*. Grand Rapids, MI: Ministry Resources Library, 1988.

Jones, Ian F. *The Counsel of Heaven on Earth: Foundations for Biblical Christian Counseling*. Nashville, TN: Broadman & Holman, 2006.

Lake, Frank. *Clinical Theology: A Theological and Psychiatric Basis to Clinical Pastoral Care*, 2 volumes. Lexington, KY: Emeth, 2006.

MacArthur, John. *Pastoral Ministry: How to Shepherd Biblically*. Nashville, TN: Thomas Nelson, 2005.

MacArthur, John, Richard Mayhue, and Robert L. Thomas. *Rediscovering Pastoral Ministry: Shaping Contemporary Ministry with Biblical Mandates*. Dallas: Word Pub., 1995.

McNeill, Donald P., Douglas A. Morrison, Henri J. M. Nouwen, and Joel Filártiga. *Compassion: A Reflection on the Christian Life*. Victoria, Australia: Image, 2005.

Oglesby, William B. *Biblical Themes for Pastoral Care*. Nashville: Abingdon, 1980.

Patton, John. *Pastoral Care in Context: An Introduction to Pastoral Care*. Louisville, KY: Westminster/John Knox, 1993.

Petersen, Bruce L. *Foundations of Pastoral Care*. Kansas City, MO: Beacon Hill of Kansas City, 2007.

Stevenson-Moessner, Jeanne. *A Primer in Pastoral Care*, Creative Pastoral Care and Counseling Series. Minneapolis: Fortress, 2005.

Stone, Bryon P. *Compassionate Ministry: Theological Foundations*. Maryknoll, NY: Orbis, 1996.

Tillich, Paul. *The Theology of Pastoral Care: The Spiritual and Theological Foundations of Pastoral Care*. Washington, DC: Advisory Committee on Clinical Pastoral Education, 1958.

2

Pastoral Care at the Bedside: Dos and Don'ts

*Lord, Your love increases my sensitivity
to needy people in today's world.
I bring my prayers to You:
for those who suffer pain;
for those whose minds are disturbed;
for brilliant people who waste their abilities;
for those with great potential
but who lack the opportunity to realize it;
for those whose dreams have shattered;
for those who live behind bars;
for those who have been maimed by violence;
for those who have been disgraced and wounded
by other people's wrongdoing;
for those who have lost a loved one;
for those who are suffering from incurable diseases;
for those who face death,
especially those who face it without You.
Help me, Father, to make myself available
to those who need help,
that in practical and in spiritual ways
I may convey Your love to them.*
— Bryan Jeffery Leech (1931-), artist, worship leader

"I was sick and you visited me."
— Jesus (Matthew 25:26)

N ow that we have set the foundation for pastoral care in the previous chapter, let's build upon that foundation and discuss the actual practice of pastoral care at the bedside.

The healthcare setting is a world of the sick and suffering. It's a place where intense feelings may be expressed, like fear, anger, guilt, abandonment, and despair. Many patients and residents are experiencing a time of great spiritual and emotional need in their lives. We need to be prepared to minister to the various spiritual and emotional needs of these people who may have diverse cultural and religious backgrounds.

Spiritually, we are prepared because we have dedicated ourselves to serving the Lord at the bedside. In this setting, we need to continually ask Him to lead us (Psalm 32:8) as we seek to show His love and compassion for those who are sick and suffering.

Emotionally, we need to be prepared. We will encounter odors that may turn our stomachs. We may hear disturbing sounds of anguish. We may see things that are embarrassing, like a patient who has exposed a private part of the body. We may see things that are disgusting, like an infected wound. How will we react to such offenses to our senses?

Unfortunately, many people are uncomfortable being around sick people. The healthcare setting can be compared to being in a foreign country where the language is awkwardly unfamiliar and the sights and sounds and smells are grossly strange. Because of this, many tend to stay away. But this isolates sick and suffering people at a highly critical time in their lives—a time when loving and compassionate care is what they need most.

During a time of physical *dis-ease*, people may experience a time of growth in their emotional and spiritual lives. On the other hand, they may whither as they suffer emotionally and spiritually, and become bitter and despondent. Our response to the hurting person during this "dark night of the soul" may be the key factor in determining which road the person travels down—a journey of either healing and wholeness or of hurting and brokenness.

As a pastoral caregiver, we can come alongside and "walk" with them during their time of hurting, not attempting to find quick and easy solutions (trying to "fix it"), but simply being there—to bring comfort through our caring pastoral presence.

Remember the words of Jesus: "Come to Me, all you who labor and are heavy laden, and I will give you rest. Take My yoke upon you and learn from Me. . ." (Matthew 11:28-29). A yoke? That sounds a lot like work rather than rest. But we need to understand that this yoke is built for two. He is *alongside* us—shouldering the burden *with* us. He has not promised to eliminate the constant tug of the plow, nor has He assured us that He will make the hard ground soft. There is no guarantee that there will be no troublesome rocks in the field. But He has promised that He will be there to *share* the difficult burdens we face. That is why He can promise that His "yoke is *easy*, and [His] burden is *light*" (verse 30, emphasis added). This is not because He has totally eliminated the problems so there will be no suffering. This is because He is there sharing the burden because He cares. Jesus has promised to give us the strength we need to endure whatever trials we might encounter.

This is what we, as a pastoral caregiver, can be when we come alongside those who are sick and suffering: Burden Bearers.[1] In fact, this is exactly what Paul tells Christians to do in Galatians 6:2, "Bear one another's burdens, and so fulfill the law of Christ."

Hurting people need to know that someone cares about them. This is especially true when the heavy burden upon their shoulders is a load that could crush them unless there are helping hands to help share the hardship. The presence of a dependable, caring person at one's bedside is perceived as supportive even though that support consists in nothing more than quietly and empathically being with the one who is facing suffering.

As a pastoral burden-bearer, are we prepared to give the patient or resident our full attention? William Justice, a hospital Chaplain for thirty-one years, makes the following suggestions to better hear what hurting people have to say to us in his book *Training Guide for Visiting the Sick*.[2] He recommends that we avoid:

- *Being too hurried.* Visit when we have time to really listen.
- *Having too much on our mind.* Clear our mind before we walk into the person's presence. Focus on understanding what the other person expresses as important to him/her.
- *Feeling too self-assured.* We may believe we already know what the client needs to hear before the person actually tells us his or her felt needs or concerns.
- *Making decisions too quickly.* We do not know what advice to give to people until we have heard them fully express themselves.
- *Allowing a personality clash.* We don't have to like everybody and not everybody is going to like us. However, never argue in the sickroom. Always show loving respect.
- *Becoming distracted by words or subjects.* We may find it easy to become diverted to our own interests by the client's words.
- *Lacking faith in the saving work of Christ.* Some tend to see Christ's salvation as relating only to some blessing beyond the grave. However, as we know from experience, He can "save from discouragement by providing encouragement, from loneliness by reminding of his presence, from guilt by giving forgiveness, and from despair by giving hope."[3]

Practical Guidelines

Several years ago a young boy received his first model car for Christmas. He was ecstatic! He ripped into the box expecting to see a nicely put together model car resembling the picture that was on the front of the box. However, what he found were hundreds of plastic pieces. His countenance sank. He looked at his dad with searching eyes that asked, "How do I do this? What do I do now?" With fatherly pleasure, his dad was able to introduce his son to a large illustrated piece of paper referred to as the "Directions."

When all else fails, follow the directions. What is true for building model cars is also true in pastoral caregiving. When all else fails, follow the directions.

For those who desire to render effective ministry to the sick and suffering—the acutely ill, the chronically ill, the terminally ill—it is necessary to follow certain good manners, with loving-kindness, compassion and wisdom, so that we will actually help rather than hinder the healing process. What follows is a list of guidelines. It includes dos and don'ts collected over the years that have been proven by the test of time and experience. They are very practical. They range from the obvious to the not so evident. But above all, they work as we come alongside the sick and suffering.

Before Entering the Room

1. Spend some time in spiritual preparation prior to the day's visits. As the old, wise saying goes: "Before talking to people about God, talk to God about people." We would never think of entering the pulpit without spending some time in prayer. Likewise, healthcare visits are an equally important ministry. Besides praying for those new contacts we will make today, it might be helpful to also offer a prayer for the special needs of the patients (or residents) whom we have seen previously.
2. Pay attention to our own personal appearance (our breath, clothes, spirit, attitude, smile, etc.). Be easy on cologne or perfume since many patients and residents are sensitive to heavy scents.
3. If we are sick, we shouldn't visit the sick.
4. Respect the need for quietness. Noise is often an irritant to those who are sick.
5. Before entering the room, glance at the light above the door. If it is on, the patient is probably asking for assistance. If so, the next person they expect to see is the nurse, not us. Therefore, do not enter.
6. Look for posted signs that may give us special information about this patient or resident.

- "No Visitors" means exactly what it says. Check with the nurse about why it was placed there. We may need to come back later.
- "Do Not Enter" may mean that the patient or resident is bathing or receiving medical care that requires privacy. Come back later.
- The "Isolation" sign is placed there for someone's protection. It may mean the person is contagious and we will need to wear protective gear before entering the room to protect ourselves. It may mean the person's resistance to infection is low and we will need to wear protective gear to protect the person from being exposed to germs. Check with the nurse and follow the instructions carefully so that everyone will be safe.
- "NPO" stands for *nil per os*, which is Latin for "nothing by mouth." Therefore, we will refrain from giving the person anything to eat or drink, even if the client asks for it (that includes the communion elements).
- "✿ Caution: Radioactivity or High-Radioactive Area" is placed outside a room of a client receiving radioactive treatment. It does not mean we can't enter the room. Find a nurse and ask what precautions need to be taken while visiting the person. Follow these instructions in order to be safe.
- "Fall Precautions" means that the client is in danger of falling if s/he gets out of bed without assistance. If the person wants to get out of bed while we are there, we need to ask for assistance from the nurse.

7. Always knock before entering the room, especially if the door is closed. We are about to enter the client's "bedroom." Common courtesy demands that, even if the door is open, we knock, announce ourselves, and wait to be invited in. Always get verbal permission from the person behind the curtain before going around a closed curtain. It may be drawn for privacy.
8. If we should have any question about whether or not to enter the room, see the nurse.

9. Be courteous to everyone we meet in the hallway.
10. Set aside any negative emotions from previous visits or experiences that we might have had. As much as possible, be one hundred percent *present* with each client.
11. Be familiar with God's purposes for illness and suffering. It's not always related to sin.
12 Try to visit a patient facing surgery the night before, or at least immediately before the surgery. Most people are anxious about their surgery.[4]
13. Our phones should be on vibrate (and we ignore any calls) or they should be turned off.
14. As we learn new pastoral care skills and hone previous skills, remember this: Our proficiency at pastoral care is dung in comparison with having Christ as the core object of our identity (Philippians 3:7-9). Make our pursuit of "excellence" in pastoral care subservient to our faith and piety. Excellence in pastoral care is good as long as it serves faith. Therefore, there is no problem with excellence per se, but when excellence becomes master, it can take on demoniac proportions in terms of distorting our motives, our energy in striving to care, and our ministry priorities. There is a story that illustrates this relationship between professional excellence and our true identity. After India's revolt, and on the day of British de-occupation, Prime Minister Nehru said to the British ambassador:

Mr. Ambassador, you must go now. But when you are twenty miles off shore, if it happens that you turn around, come back and say, "We wish to serve you, India," then you are most welcome. But if you come and say, "We wish to be master again," then you must go, and go for good.

In Nehru's language, excellence must "go" unless it serves growth in our true identity in Jesus Christ.

During the Visit

1. If the client is asleep, we need to check with the nurse to see if we should awaken the person or let him/her sleep. If unable to visit, it would be good to leave a brief note by the bedside.
2. Take note of the details in the room. Flowers, cards and balloons may give an indication of the amount of attention and support the patient or resident may be receiving from family and friends.
3. Take note of the client: What is our first impression? Does the person seem to be emotionally up or down? Is the person reading, watching TV, or doing nothing? What do these clues tell you?
4. Be sensitive and courteous to others in the room: patients/residents, family, other visitors, and the healthcare staff.
5. Go behind curtains only with permission. Even though we may have been invited into the room, wait until we are invited to go behind the curtain. Simply ask, "May I come behind the curtain?"
6. Feel free to draw the curtain if it is a semi-private room. The curtain is there for privacy.
7. According to Proverbs 25:20, it is important to be sensitive to a person's frame of mind. We need to make appropriate adjustments within ourselves to the mood and tone of the client. We need to try to gauge where the patient or resident is emotionally, and then bend our response to where the person is at the moment. As Romans 12:15 advises, we should laugh with those who are happy and share tears with those who are weeping.
8. Show genuine concern through our facial expression. A warm smile tends to brighten any room. Be cheerful without acting the clown or joker.
9. Be thoughtful about our initial moments in the room. We set the tone. Be naturally friendly. Greet the individual warmly.
10. If the patient or resident is unknown to us, address the person as Mr. or Ms. Many cultures think it disrespectful to call an elder by his or her first name.

11. Always let the client take the lead in shaking hands. If they do offer their hand, be gentle, only applying the same amount of pressure that they do.
12. Don't sit on the bed unless it is appropriate to do so and we receive permission from the patient or resident and the nurse. To sit on the bed is to invade the client's private space. In addition, realize that sitting on the bed can tighter the covers around the person's body, it can obstruct tubes, and the movement can be uncomfortable for the person.
13. Be aware of where to stand or sit. Make sure that it is in line with the client's vision, not against a bright light or window and close enough to be able to touch the person if necessary and appropriate. We shouldn't make the person twist or strain to see us.
14. Pull up a chair and sit down near the bedside. To remain standing may communicate that we are in a hurry and have more important things to do than stay and talk with them. Give the person our full and undivided attention.
15. Be aware of the special equipment that might be in the room or on the floor so that we don't interfere with it or step on tubes.
16. Be careful not to act shocked at their appearance. If we can't help it, say something vague like, "Well, you really got shaken up." Try to move on to center the conversation on the person and how s/he is coping.
17. State who we are (name and title) and why we are there. Remember our purpose—our pastoral care role—for coming alongside the bedside.
18. Begin with the patient or resident at the point of his/her concern. Let the person tell us what his/her concern is. A simple question like, "How are things going?" can usually get the person talking.
19. Don't force the conversation. Focus the discussion on the client and his/her world. Sometimes a general observation about what s/he has been doing or reading or watching may be helpful to get the dialogue flowing.
20. Let them express their feelings and/or anger at what God may be teaching them. If we sense that they are upset, we might gently point that out. To get them started in this direction we

might say, "You know, sometimes God has a way of using illness to teach us important principles about life. Have you found that true in your experience?"

21. Be positive. There are enough negative experiences going on in the person's life. However, don't give false hope, such as saying, "Everything will be all right." Always give hope, but always keep it within the realm of reality.

22. Be a good listener. Be honest without being brutal. Be sympathetic without being morbid.

23. Our conversation with the patient or resident should be private—between us and the person. Do not give counsel loudly so that others may be preached at, as it were, at the same time. This doesn't mean we need to whisper; a normal voice is fine. Remember, we are there to comfort. Obviously, if the person is hard of hearing, then we must speak loudly.

24. Don't diagnose or tell somebody else's (or our own) experience concerning this illness.

25. Don't be drawn into criticism or try to second-guess the doctors or nurses.

26. Be sensitive to the person's degree of awareness concerning his/her diagnosis and prognosis—the person may be in denial, unaware, or lack understanding of the details.

27. Be careful not to belittle or minimize the person's illness. Some operations are minor or routine to everyone except the person being operated on.[5]

28. We need to be careful not to take our theology too far and second-guess God as to why this person is experiencing a trial. Saying something like, "It's difficult to understand why this happened, but I want to reassure you that you're not alone while you're going through this," is far more important than being guilty of giving easy or unwanted advice.

29. Don't hesitate to share Scripture and to pray when it's appropriate to do so. But don't force prayer or spiritual resources on any individual. If we're aware of a Bible verse we think might be helpful to the person, we might ask, "Would you like me to read something from the Bible that relates to what we've been talking about?" If it seems appropriate to pray, we might ask, "Would it be all right to pray with you now,

or would you prefer that I remember you later in my own private prayers?" Many patients will respect you for leaving the option up to them.

30. When appropriate to do so, use the opportunity to share the Gospel. However, always be respectful of those who have a different belief system from our own. Never impose our faith on someone else, which would be unethical pastoral care.

31. We need to adjust the length of our visit to the needs of the patient or resident. Patients (and some residents) often tire easily. A relaxed visit of ten to fifteen minutes may be adequate. There is only one reason to stay longer: the person is prolonging the visit concerning a subject important to him or her.

32. Understand our personal and professional limits. If needed, make an appropriate referral to someone more knowledgeable or skilled at dealing with the client's concerns.

33. To argue is inexcusable. Controversy on any subject will neither heal nor win the heart.

34. Accept interruptions.

   ▪ If medical personnel enter the room to give a treatment, we can tell the person we will either wait outside or come back later.

   ▪ Offer to come back later when meals are served. Food shoved aside until we leave will be cold and unappetizing later (and that may make them resent our visit).

   ▪ Offer to leave if the person receives a phone call. We can ask, "Would you like for me to step out while you're on the phone, or would you prefer that I stay?"

35. Try not to disturb others in the room. If they are awake, greet them when coming and leaving. Be alert to opportunities for pastoral care ministry in these situations.

36. When visiting in the ICU or CCU, we should make our stay with the patient short (about 5 minutes). Use the visit primarily as a time to minister to the family.

37. Try to be sensitive to possible embarrassments, pain, nausea, or drowsiness that can be caused by the illness or the drugs

administered to the patient or resident. Medication has various effects upon people. It may change or alter their normal personality. In some cases they will not even remember that we visited.

38. Be careful about what we do and say in the presence of a client who appears to be in a coma. They may be hearing what we say.

39. Be sensitive to the family as well as the patient or resident. Effective ministry can be made to family members and friends during an illness.

40. Be sensitive to possible ministry to the staff.

41. Be careful not to over commit ourselves. Perhaps we could make other arrangements for assistance or find someone who would help do what is needed. Churches with Stephen Ministry programs have qualified people who often assist individuals. Enlist their help. Many needs can also be met by a social worker. Make a referral.

42. For a serious surgery, offer to stay with the family.

43. Visits to patients immediately following major surgery should be especially brief.

44. Remember that we have a unique opportunity to share God's love and compassion in a very practical way.

45. When we are ready to leave, leave. Don't prolong the exit.

46. Promise a return visit only if we are certain we will return.

After the Visit

1. We should wash our hands, especially if we touched the patient or resident. Healthcare facilities are loaded with contagious germs. Washing hands protects ourselves and the people we will visit next.

2. When appropriate (and with the person's permission), make a referral to social services, a professional counselor, or a Pastor.

3. When the patient goes home, depending on the ministry that we had with the person, we might want to check up on him/her by phone (as long as it is not against the policy of the healthcare facility to do so). Make sure to get the patient's permission to call. Some overlook this meaningful follow-up ministry.

4. We need to continue to pray for our patients or residents and their family members.

Evaluating the Visit

It is always a good idea to take a moment to reflect on how our visit went to see if there might be any lessons we can learn in order to improve our pastoral care skills. We might want to ask ourselves some of the following questions:

1. Was the time of my call convenient for the person, or did I do it when it was merely convenient for me?
2. Did I feel welcome? Why or why not?
3. How much of the conversation centered on me rather than the client?
4. How much talking did I do? Did I dominate the conversation or did I let the person share his or her thoughts and feelings without interruption or imposing my own agenda?
5. How was the length of my visit appropriate?
6. Did I control the subject matter or did I let the person choose the topics?
7. How was the Scripture I shared pertinent to the person's situation? Did I receive permission to share Scripture or did I impose it on the person?
8. In what ways was my prayer personal and relevant to the person's specific needs? Did I receive permission to pray with the person or did I force prayer on the person?
9. Did I know when it was time to leave, or did I sit and hunt for more to say?
10. How was the visit helpful to this person?
11. What did I identify as the client's spiritual needs? How were these needs met? If they were not met, how do I plan on meeting them in the future?

Qualities of a Good Pastoral Caregiver

Now that we've studied a few dos and don'ts regarding visiting the sick and suffering, it's important to remember that pastoral caregiving has more to do with *who* we are than *what* we do. The following are some characteristics of a quality pastoral caregiver.

- **Available** — willing to give of our time, talents and gifts to serve others.
- **Approachable** — willing to be a bridge-builder rather than a wall-builder.
- **Attentive** — willing to listen with our heart as well as our ears.
- **Affirming** — willing to encourage and build up others with our supportive presence and words.
- **Assuring** — willing to give a glimpse of hope and give positive words of comfort from the promises of God.
- **Authentic** — willing to be open and honest.

Questions for Review

1. What are some important guidelines to consider before entering a patient's or resident's room?
2. Can you name some key guidelines to keep in mind during the pastoral care visit?
3. What should you do after the visit?
4. What are some questions to ask in evaluating your visit?

Questions for Reflection

1. Take some time in Bible study, reflection and prayer about being available, approachable, attentive, affirming, assuring, and authentic. In what ways are these character traits an important part of who you are and what you do as a pastoral caregiver? Record your insights and share them with a confidant and/or the training team.
2. If you have ever been a patient, reflect on how you were treated and how you responded to that treatment. What

was least helpful? What was most meaningful? How will this knowledge impact your pastoral care? Record your thoughts in a journal and share your insights with a confidant and/or the training team.

3. Read the following passages of Scripture: Matthew 9:36; Mark 1:41; 8:1-3; Luke 7:11-13; Philippians 2:1-11; 1 Thessalonians 2:1-12. After spending several minutes in Bible study, reflection and prayer, make observations about the personal qualities Jesus and the Apostle Paul exhibited in ministering to others. Record your insights and share them with a confidant and/or the training team.

Chapter Resources

Biddle, Perry H., Jr. *A Hospital Visitation Manual*, Grand Rapids, MI: Wm. B. Eerdmans Pub., 1994.

Champlin, Joseph M., and Susan C. Taylor. *A Thoughtful Word, A Healing Touch: A Guide for Visiting the Sick*. Mystic, CT: Twenty-third Pub., 1995.

Croft, Brian. *Visit the Sick: Ministering God's Grace in Times of Illness*. Leominster, UK: DayOne Pub., 2008.

Dayringer, Richard. *Pastor and Patient: A Handbook for Clergy Who Visit the Sick*. New York: Jason Aronson, 1995.

Dicks, Russell L. *How to Make Pastoral Calls*. St. Louis: Bethany, 1962.

Gorsuck, Nancy J. *Pastoral Visitation*. Minneapolis: Fortress, 1999.

Grantham, Rudolph E. *Lay Shepherding: A Guide for Visiting the Sick, the Aged, the Troubled and the Bereaved*. Valley Forge, PA: Judson, 1980.

Handler, Jane, Kim Heatherington, and Rabbi Stuart L. Kellman. *Give Me Your Hand: Traditional and Practical Guidance of Visiting the Sick*, 2nd ed. Oakland, CA: Eks Pub., 1998.

Just, Arthur A., Jr., and Scot A. Kinnaman, eds. *Visitation: Resources for the Care of Souls*. St. Louis, MO: Concordia Pub. House, 2007.

Justice, William G. *Training Guide for Visiting the Sick: More than a Social Call*. New York: Haworth Pastoral, 2005.

Kirkendoll, Michael L. *The Hospital Visit: A Pastor's Guide.* Nashville: Abingdon, 2001.

Kirkwood, Neville D. *Pastoral Care in Hospitals.* Harrisburg, PA: Morehouse Pub., 1999.

Maxwell, Katie. *Bedside Manners: A Practical Guide to Visiting the Ill.* Grand Rapids, MI: Baker, 2005.

McCall, Junietta Baker. *A Practical Guide to Hospital Ministry: Healing Ways.* New York: Haworth Pastoral, 2002.

Normile, Patti. *Visiting the Sick: A Guide for Parish Ministers.* Cincinnati, OH: St. Anthony Messenger, 1992.

Oemler, Christian. *The Pastor at the Sick Bed.* Philadelphia, PA: Grigg and Elliot, 1936.

Patton, John. *Pastoral Care: An Essential Guide.* Nashville: Abingdon, 2005.

Reimer, Lawrence D., James T. Wagner, and Wayne E. Oates. *The Hospital Handbook: A Practical Guide to Hospital Visitation.* Wilton, CT: Morehouse Barlow, 1984.

Richmond, Kent D., and David L. Middleton. *The Pastor and the Patient: A Practical Guidebook for Hospital Visitation.* Nashville: Abingdon, 1992.

Saylor, Dennis. *A Guide to Hospital Calling for Deacons, Elders and Other Laypersons.* Grand Rapids, MI: Baker Book House, 1983.

Weir, William. *Visiting the Sick and Elderly.* Rock Hill, SC: Overcomer, 1997.

3

Empathic Listening

The saddest part about being human is not paying attention.
Presence is the gift of life.
— Stephen Levine (1942-), poet, author, teacher[1]

Man's inability to communicate is a result of
his failure to listen effectively.
— Carl Rogers (1902-1987), American psychologist[2]

The greatest compliment that was ever paid me
was when one asked me what I thought,
and attended to my answer.
— Henry David Thoreau (1817-1862),
American author, naturalist[3]

You must all be quick to listen, slow to speak.
— James (James 1:19, NLT)

P atients frequently thank pastoral caregivers for listening to them. This compliment about listening is given to them more often than for any other ministry activity they do. Very few on the healthcare staff seem to have much time to listen attentively to their clients. In fact, one of the greatest complaints by patients is that no one takes time to hear what they urgently want to say. Sometimes, after introducing myself as the Chaplain, a patient will ask, "What do you want to say to me?" They show great joy when I respond with, "My only agenda is to consider whatever interests you." Nothing is appreciated as much as the importance we show to another through listening.

Terry Felber, an author and speaker on communication, says:

Active listening communicates sincere interest more effectively than anything else you can do. Active listening means taking the time and effort to really hear the intent of the person communicating with you.[4]

Being Heard = Being Loved

One of our great challenges in ministry is loving people, especially when they are not so loveable. But Jesus mandated that we should love our neighbor (Mark 12:28-31). And one way we can demonstrate love for people is by listening to them.

David Augsburger, author and professor, has said,

Being heard *is so close to* being loved *that for the average person they are almost indistinguishable. . .Within each human person there is a deep need to be heard as a real person, a person of importance who merits attention and respect.*[5]

Listening attentively to a person in crisis is a powerful way of communicating loving care for that person. Listening communicates to a person that s/he is valued and loved. And as we love them by listening to them, we give a person in crisis an opportunity to reflect about what has happened, what it might mean, and what s/he may need to do in response to the situation. And listening gives the person in crisis an opportunity to share his/her thoughts, feelings, concerns, and needs with someone who is willing to share the pain through empathic listening.

Listening is a fine art that requires a heart of love and compassion, a willingness to risk relationship, and a readiness to share pain.

Listening = Practical Theology

Another pastoral care challenge we face is applying our theological understanding to everyday life. The Greek word for theology is literally translated: "to talk about God." Practical theology is an attempt to integrate this God talk with our daily walk. What better ways to do this than to listen to people tell their stories about how God is part of their journey. I think that's what Mary Pellauer had in mind when she wrote, "If there's anything worth calling *theology*, it is *listening* to people's stories—*listening* to them and honoring and cherishing them. . ."[6]

Listening is where the rubber tire of theology meets the bumpy road of life.

Listening = Caring

The ability to show that we really do care about people is another challenge we face in ministry to the hurting. Henri Nouwen, in an article he wrote on "Care of the Elderly," stated his conviction that "*Listening* is a very active and extremely alert form of *caring*."[7]

Listening is tuning in to another person even when that person can't articulate what s/he is thinking or feeling, which is not so uncommon for someone sick in a hospital bed or going through some other crisis. Empathic listening accepts people as they are—whether reckless, ill-tempered, distressed or joyful—and it lovingly explores these feelings with them.[8]

When pastoral caregivers really listen, healing of emotional and spiritual pain can take place. Listening to people is, indeed, an active form of caring.

Listening = Doing

When we often talk about pastoral care, it's usually about what we can *do*. It's about tangible expressions of care. So we talk about holding a hand, bringing a meal, quoting a verse, singing a song, mowing a lawn, praying a prayer, driving an errand, or some other *activity* of caring. For Juanita Ryan, who gives some vital and practical insights on how to help people going through a crisis in her book *Standing By*, she says, "*Listening* is the beginning point for *doing*."[9]

Listening *is* doing something helpful for hurting people. Listening is *doing* pastoral care.

Listening = Message

As pastoral caregivers, I would think that all of us want to share the healing truths from the Word of God. We tend to place a lot of value on speaking God's truth and applying it to life situations. Like the Apostle Peter, we are convinced that the living Word has words of life and we want to share His Word with those in need of His transforming and healing words of life (John 6:68).

I think that most of us in ministry tend to place more value on speaking than on listening. That's often the primary focus as we go through seminary. At least that's the way I saw it when I was a seminary student and young pastor. However, Ken Sharp, president of Rapha Christian Counseling Center, makes this poignant statement: "The awesome power of the *listening ear* equates to the power of the *spoken word*."[10]

I find it interesting that Organization Strategy Institute claims: "Inadequate listening skills waste approximately 80% of organizational resources." The problem, from their viewpoint, was not that people weren't speaking clearly or that the subject wasn't important, but the problem was that people weren't listening carefully to what was actually being said.[11]

Listening, in and of itself, is a message. And that message says we care. Listening is at the heart of the pastoral care message.

Empathic Listening: What is it?

Why do we call it "empathic" listening? First of all, it's because we're *hearing with the intent to **understand** rather than to reply*. In other words, we're not waiting for them to stop talking so that we can give them *our* words of wisdom or tell them *our* viewpoint. Instead we restrain the impulse to offer hasty advice or pass quick judgment because we're trying to understand *their* point of view first.

Second, it's empathic listening because we're *concentrating with our **heart*** (which includes the mind as well as the emotions) *as well as our **eyes** and **ears***. We are fully focused on the person with our whole being. I don't know about you, but for me that takes tremendous concentrative effort. Empathic listening is not *casual* listening but *active* listening that is fully engaged with the other person.

Finally, empathic listening is *seeking to understand the patient **first**, before I am understood*. That means I'm listening to the person in order to *learn* rather than to teach. I'm first of all a *student* before trying to be an instructor or guidance counselor.

Empathic Listening: How do I do it?

So how do we do empathic listening? Let me suggest that we practice the following five steps:

First, *tune in to God's Spirit*. As we know, pastoral care is a spiritual ministry. It involves the soul. Therefore, we must be sensitive to God's leading and listen to Him. Remember the counsel of Zechariah 4:6? *It is not by force nor by strength, but by my Spirit, says the LORD Almighty* (NLT).

Good pastoral care is not so much about our professional credentials or ministry skills, it's not about our persuasive counsel or flawless techniques (don't get me wrong, all of these are important aspects of good pastoral care), but it's primarily about yielding to God's Spirit and allowing Him to work in and through us to accomplish His will.

We first of all tune into God's Spirit and, second, we *tune out our own agenda*. We don't really know what they need from us until we first hear what they have to say. We're not as open to listen if we already have a spiritual care plan established in our minds for them. That doesn't mean it's wrong to be prepared with a spiritual care plan for different problems (like depression, grief, divorce, etc.). It simply means we don't implement that plan until *after* they tell us that is exactly what they really need and want from us.

At the same time that we tune out our own agenda, we also *tune in to our senses*. What are our senses (our eyes and ears—physical senses—along with our heart and mind—spiritual senses) telling us about the real (and often hidden) message we're receiving?

To be empathic listeners we must also try to *tune out distractions*. What are some potential distractions? They include what we hear them saying (the subject), what we hear going on around us (another conversation or beeping machines), what we're looking at (IV tubes, TV, unpleasant sights), what we're smelling (gross odors), and what we're thinking (rambling thoughts). In fact, our self-talk may be one of our biggest distractions.

Finally, empathic listening means that we *tune in to their message*. We focus our full attention on what the person is trying to tell us. That includes what is not being said (the non-verbal message through tone of voice and posture and facial expressions).

Empathic Listening: It's a Biblical Process

They have a part in the listening process, and, according to James 5:16, that part is to *confess*. To confess simply means to tell or make known one's thoughts and feelings; to disclose one's faults and shortcomings; to unburden one's transgressions; or simply to share the state of one's conscience. And people are more willing to do this when there is someone who is willing to listen—to care—without interrupting them with critical or judgmental comments or giving unasked for advice.

Our part in the process is seen in three verses from the Bible: *Everyone should be quick to listen, slow to speak. . .* (James 1:19, NIV). We normally do the opposite of this. We are often swift to speak and offer our unasked for opinions in order to try to quickly fix the problem while being slow to take the time to really listen to their heart. We are encouraged by this verse to take time to listen to people tell their stories. We are admonished to hesitate, through listening, before we do offer our advice. It doesn't say we should never offer any counsel (see also Ecclesiastes 3:1, 7b). Making a comment is only inappropriate if we have not been quick to listen to the whole story.

To answer before listening—that is folly and shame (Proverbs 18:13, NIV). This tells us that it is disgraceful to give an answer before we hear what the issue is. We are guilty of foolish behavior when we interrupt someone who is talking in order to tell them what we think they need to hear before fully letting them explain. Again, there is a time and place for pastoral counsel. But this counsel must come only after first of all taking the time to empathically listen.

The heart of the discerning acquires knowledge, for the ears of the wise seek it out (Proverbs 18:15, NIV). Notice that this verse says the *ears* of the wise—not the *minds* of the wise—seek out insights. Why? Because this is the tool and attitude of a learner and discerner who listens to what others have to say so we can better understand them. We gather from without (through the ears) in order to understand within (the heart). The ears are the channels for gaining knowledge and understanding. Knowledge and wisdom come from listening.

As pastoral caregivers, one of our roles is to be a *burden-bearer*. How is *listening* part of the burden-bearing process (see Galatians 6:2)? Listening allows us to learn what the burdens are. We understand through hearing what is weighing down the person and causing them distress. Listening gives us clues that will help us know how to come alongside and help lift and carry that burden with them.

Job asked his "counselors" to stop talking and really pay attention to his arguments (Job 13:5-6, 13; and compare with 2:13). Job simply and clearly declares that people who are suffering want their story to be heard. And when that doesn't happen, he goes on to emphatically declare, "What miserable comforters you are!" (Job 16:2, NLT).

The Listening Process and Healing

I would like for us to look afresh at James 5:16 from this perspective of providing empathic listening to those who are hurting. In this passage, the sick person calls for the Elders of the Church. When they arrive, the sick person "confesses"—tells them what's going on in his or her life. We can assume these pastoral caregivers empathically listen to the person's story. The person feels understood as the elders fully listen to him/her and they, because they're empathically listening, have a better understanding about what's really going on in the person's life. This means the elders are able to pray more effectively for the person who is sick. And as a result, the sick person experiences "healing"—both physical and spiritual wholeness/wellness—as a result of this effective pastoral care, which began with coming alongside to empathically listen to someone tell his or her personal story.

What Do You Do With What You Hear?

Solomon said that there's "a time to keep silence [to listen], and a time to speak [give counsel]" (Ecclesiastes 3:7b). So what do we do with what we hear? There are three things I don't want us to do:

First, we need to avoid being critical of people based on what they say. Condemning the person is God's role, not ours. Pastoral caregiving does not involve being judgmental (cf. Matthew 7:1-5).

Second, we need to try to avoid overreacting too emotionally to what we hear. Hearing criticism or strong emotions can cause us to overreact by becoming defensive. For example, we don't need to tell them, "You shouldn't feel that way," when they share some strong feelings. Having a strong emotional reaction to a tough situation is normal.

Finally, we need to stay away from preaching at people because of what they have said. Pastoral caregiving in the midst of a crisis is usually not a time for *correction*; it's primarily a time to *comfort* the person. Does this mean we agree with everything they say? Certainly not! It is possible to be consoling without agreeing with wrong beliefs.

There are two things that I do want us to do:

First, we *care* for them. The word "care" in 1 Corinthians 12:25 is from the Greek root *merizō*, which means to be drawn in different directions, to be distracted. It is an anxious care. What does that mean? (Compare 1 Peter 5:7 and Philippians 4:6-7.) I think it means that in the process of listening we actually get what the person is saying (and feeling) so well that it affects us. If they are suffering, we suffer. If they are rejoicing, we rejoice. We really care.

Second, we *empathize* with (*einfühlung*: "feeling into") them. Remember: It's God's responsibility to rescue them, not ours. So we don't need to take things into our own hands. We don't need to "fix it."

Communicating Care by Listening: Basic Principles[12]

Attending. This is giving our full attention to someone. How do we do that? By leaning toward them, showing interest in what they're talking about, giving good eye-contact, and responding so as to encourage further sharing. We can do this by giving feedback of content *plus* feelings.

Being Silent. Silence gives them time to think. We need to try not to interrupt their quiet reflection with hasty words. We need to become comfortable with pauses. According to Wayne Oates, psychologist and educator:

> *The reality of silence is no mere "gimmick" for manipulating people. For it to be meaningful, a listening silence must transcend the dreary fate of being a "technique" of pastoral counseling. It becomes a spiritual discipline of patience, prayer, and longsuffering in "waiting before God."*[13]

Reflecting. This is providing a "mirror." It involves saying in fresh words what s/he seems to be feeling. For example, "That seems to frustrate you," or "You sound like you feel guilty over what happened." It can also involve the restatement of thoughts. For example, "You seem to be having a hard time understanding why this had to happen," or "It appears to me that you think what happened isn't fair." We can also reflect a description of behavior. For example, "You appear rather tense about this right now," or "You're smiling on the outside, but I'm wondering if you're really hurting on the inside."

The purpose of reflecting on what has been said is not so much for us to gain more information, but to encourage the person to clarify his/her thoughts and feelings about the problem. Reflecting communicates our full attention and our willingness to share in the pain of their crisis.

Responding to Feelings. This is giving value to emotions. Some of us, and I'm speaking mostly about myself here, work hard to communicate facts and ideas, but are less skilled in communicating about emotional realities. We need to listen for "feeling" words and feeling tones in the voice, as well as non-verbal indicators of feelings, and then we respond to them on a feeling level so they might explore their feelings more fully.

Asking Questions. This helps to identify what has happened, to understand their thoughts and feelings, and to determine what is needed to help alleviate their spiritual distress. Using open-ended questions, like "Tell me more," can be helpful. We should avoid asking "why" questions of people in the midst of a crisis. They may not fully understand the why of what's going on at this time.

Clarifying. This is making sure we have accurately under-stood them. Clarifying is repeating back to the person what we have heard. The process of clarifying serves as a check on our understanding of what has been communicated. It keeps the focus on the experience of the person in crisis. It gives the person an opportunity to hear a "tape" of his/her communication played back, giving the person important feedback and an opportunity to reconsider or further explain his/her experience and understanding.

Summarizing. This is putting closure on a conversation. This provides an opportunity to give direct reassurance of our care in the context of all that has been shared. Praying for their specific concerns can be a very meaningful way to summarize the strug-gles of the crisis in the context of God's care. On prayer, Juanita Ryan makes this meaningful comment:

A final caring response we can offer a friend in crisis is to pray for him. In the past I have often heard people respond to a need with a half-sincere "I'll pray for you." Such responses are often equivalent to saying, "be warmed and filled" without doing anything tangible to respond to the expressed need. As a consequence I used to avoid telling people I would pray for them. But I have learned that praying for someone after listening to them with empathy is one of the greatest gifts we can possibly give to a person in crisis. People in crisis often have enormous needs. They cannot find a job. Their child is in trouble with the law. They are faced with death and grief. We can give them the gift of listening, we can share their pain, but we cannot get them a job or protect their son or go with them into death. Our own resources are inadequate to meet the needs. But God has called us to come to him to request his help and protection and presence. To be obedient to him and to be faithful to our friend we must respond in prayer for him. At times it might be appropriate to ask our friend if he would like us to pray for him while we are with him. If he would like us to pray we should be honest in our prayer, stating simply and specifically his needs and concerns, and asking God to give him the help or healing or protection that is needed.[14]

Why is it so Hard to Listen? And What to Do About It

Here are some basic reasons why it is so hard for us to sometimes listen empathically to people as we're coming alongside them:

We make assumptions. We think we know what the person is going to say so we don't listen and tend to interrupt to fill in the gaps or jump to our own conclusions. Instead, we need to listen with an open mind that waits to respond until we've heard the whole story.

We have biases. The person's outward appearance or lifestyle or opinions block us from truly hearing what is being said. If we do have a prejudiced thought, we need to try not to focus on it by trying to see the person from God's perspective.

We like to be in control of the conversation. We feel the need to interrupt or correct in order to stay in control of the direction of the visit. Instead, we need to try to let go of our own agenda and listen with our heart to their story.

There are many distractions that make it hard for us to listen. It's easy to lose our attentiveness primarily because we think so much faster than they can talk. One way to try to stay in the moment is by making good eye contact.

Finally, our ego can get in the way. We can change the focus of attention to ourselves rather than the client. How do we do that? One way is when we tell our own personal stories, which result in changing the attention from the client to us.

Nonverbal Communication

Here are some ways that nonverbal actions communicate:

Yawning may say that I'm tired of listening to you; I'm bored.

Crossed arms tend to communicate that I'm not open to what they have to say. However, it may simply mean that the person is cold.

Looking at my watch may imply that I think they've talked too long or that I have something more important to do.

Tapping my fingers or pen, which may simply be a nervous habit, may also communicate that I'm irritated with the subject or how long they have been talking and I want them to hurry up and finish.

Frowning may say that I don't agree with them or I'm not sure they know what they're talking about.

Gazing around may communicate that what they're saying isn't important to me or I'm not interested in what they have to say.

Tightening my jaw could mean that I disagree with them or that I want them to hurry up and finish so I can talk.

Raising my eyebrows could communicate that I think they're getting carried away or that I don't understand.

Coming near usually says that I care and want to hear what they have to say; while *staying distant* could imply that I don't really care or want to listen.

Suddenly leaning forward may say that I really want to hear what they have to say while leaning away may communicate that I'm done listening.

How Would You Describe Yourself as a Listener?

You need to take some time to reflect on each of the following questions:

When someone is talking, do you find it difficult to keep your mind from wandering to other things?

When you're listening to someone, do you go beyond the facts being discussed and try to sense how s/he is feeling about the matter?

Do certain subjects or phrases prejudice you so that you can't objectively listen to what is being said?

When you're puzzled or annoyed by what someone says, do you try to get the question straightened out as soon as possible?

If you feel it would take too much time and effort to understand something, do you go out of your way to avoid hearing about it?

When someone is talking, do you try to make them think you're paying attention when you're really not?

When you're listening to another person, are you easily distracted by nearby sights and sounds?

Questions for Review

1. How would you describe empathic listening?
2. Why is empathic listening important in coming alongside people who are in crisis?
3. What are some basic principles of listening that communicate you care?
4. Why is it hard for you to listen to people?

Questions for Reflection

1. Spend some time in Bible study, reflection, and prayer about your listening skills. How has listening affected you, your Christian walk, and your visitation ministry? Record your insights in a journal and discuss them with a confidant and/or the training team.
2. Watch a sit-com segment that involves 2-3 people talking together. How did the situation fit your definition of empathic listening? What elements of empathic listening did you observe? What did you learn about listening from this experience? Record your insights in a journal and discuss them with a confidant and/or the training team.
3. List one thing you can do to improve your listening habits while coming alongside the hurting. Commit to a plan for improving your listening skills over the next month. After each week of the next month, evaluate how successful your plan has been and make any appropriate adjustments. Discuss your plan with a confidant and/or the training team.

Chapter Resources

Akhtar, Salman. *Listening to Others: Developmental and Clinical Aspects of Empathy and Attunement*. Lanham: Jason Aronson, 2007.

Augsburger, David W. *Caring Enough to Hear and Be Heard*. Ventura, CA: Regal, 1982.

Barker, Larry Lee, and Kittie W. Watson. *Listen Up: How to Improve Relationships, Reduce Stress, and Be More Productive by Using the Power of Listening*. New York: St. Martin's, 2000.

Bone, Diane. *The Business of Listening: A Practical Guide to Effective Listening*. Los Altos, CA: Crisp Pub., 1988.

Brady, Mark. *Wisdom of Listening*. Boston: Wisdom Publications, 2003.

Burley-Allen, Madelyn. *Listening: The Forgotten Skill* (A Self Teaching GuideNew York: Wiley, 1982.

Coakley, Carolyn Gwynn, and Andrew D. Wolvin. *Listening.* Dubuque, IA: W. C. Brown, 1982.

Donoghue, Paul J., and Mary E. Siegel. *Are You Really Listening? Keys to Successful Communication.* Notre Dame, IN: Sorin, 2005.

Gilbert, Richard B. *Health Care & Spirituality: Listening, Assessing, Caring.* Amityville, NY: Baywood Pub., 2002.

Hart, Thomas N. *The Art of Christian Listening.* New York: Paulist, 1980.

Hedahl, Susan K. *Listening Ministry: Rethinking Pastoral Leadership.* Minneapolis: Fortress, 2001.

Hoppe, Michael H. *Active Listening: Improve Your Ability to Listen and Lead.* Greensboro, NC: Center for Creative Leadership, 2006.

Huggert, Joyce. *Listening to Others.* London, UK: Hodder and Stoughton, 1988.

Kratz, Dennis M., and Abby Robinson Kratz. *Effective Listening Skills.* Chicago: Irwin Professional Pub., 1995.

Leeds, Dorothy. *The 7 Powers of Questions: Secrets to Successful Communication in Life and at Work.* New York: Berkley Pub. Group, 2000.

Oates, Wayne E. *The Presence of God in Pastoral Counseling.* Waco, TX: Word, 1986.

Pembroke, Neil. *The Art of Listening: Dialogue, Shame, and Pastoral Care.* London: T & T Clark/Handsel, 2002.

Savage, John S. *Listening and Caring Skills in Ministry: A Guide for Pastors, Counselors, and Small Groups.* Nashville: Abingdon, 1996.

Stairs, Jean. *Listening for the Soul: Pastoral Care and Spiritual Direction.* Minneapolis: Fortress, 2000.

Sullivan, James E. *The Good Listener.* Norte Dame, IN: Ave Maria, 2000.

Taylor, Elizabeth Johnston. *What Do I Say?: Talking with Patients about Spirituality.* Philadelphia: Templeton Foundation, 2007.

4

Coming Alongside Patients and Residents

I was hungry
and you formed a humanities club to discuss my hunger.
Thank you!
I was imprisoned
and you crept off quietly to your chapel to pray for my release.
Nice!
I was naked
and in your mind you debated the morality of my appearance.
What good did that do?
I was sick
and you knelt and thanked God for your health.
But I needed you!
I was homeless
and you preached to me of the shelter of the love of God.
I wish you'd taken me home!
I was lonely
and you left me alone to pray for me.
Why didn't you stay?
You seem holy, so close to God;
but I'm still very hungry, lonely, cold, and still in pain.
Does it matter?
— Anonymous

H ave you ever tried to hammer a nail into a board with your hand? I doubt it. There would be a lot of damage done to your hand while the nail remained unmoved. Having the right tools available to complete a task is invaluable. That principle is true in Bible study and it is true in pastoral care as well.

We have been called to a ministry of coming alongside the sick and suffering. But simply grabbing the hammer and saw of good intentions is often inadequate. Sharper tools are necessary to penetrate the soil we have been called to cultivate. What tools do we need to effectively minister to the sick and suffering?

In this chapter we will examine our pastoral approach as well as the use of Scripture, prayer, and other tools that are often used in ministry.

The Pastoral Caregiver's Role

Michael Milton, Senior Pastor of First Presbyterian Church in Chattanooga, TN, shares the following true story.[1] A new Chaplain at a large hospital had on his clerical collar. He made a visit to a patient who was scheduled for surgery. The patient, a middle-aged man, frowned as he watched the Chaplain stroll in. He looked the Chaplain in the eyes and growled out, "Yeah, Chaplain, can I help you?"

The Chaplain replied, "I am the hospital Chaplain."

The patient lowered himself back into the covers. "I figured that much, Chaplain." The grumpy patient then sat up and said,

"Chaplain, tell me something. This morning the surgeon who will perform my surgery came in. He marked me all up on my chest where he plans to cut away at my breast-bone to get at my heart. I knew why he was here. Then in came a nurse. She hooked me up to these IVs. I knew why she was here. A little lady came in shortly before you arrived to fix me up with a bedpan, if I needed it. Now, I even know why she was here. But, Chaplain, the question I have of you and every other fellow like you in that dog collar is this: What in the _ _ _ _ are you doing here?"

The Chaplain stood there for a moment and then responded with, "Actually, I am here because God sent me to see you."

The Chaplain's response had a big impact on the man. He came back with:

> "Okay, Chaplain, okay, I guess I get it. All right, so I know why you are here. Pardon me for putting it the way I did, but I am the Chief of Psychiatry at this hospital and for thirty years I have always wondered why you people were here. I may not believe what you believe, but I guess I know why you think you must be here."

The Chaplain, feeling a little braver, said, "So, tell me Doctor, how are things with you and God?"

The psychiatrist was a little staggered by the question, but then relaxed and reflectively replied,

> "I will tell you this: I've seen a lot of simple operations get a little fouled up over the years. My operation will be open-heart surgery. I know full well that if something were to go wrong. . .well, I guess I'm saying. . .I'm not sure about God."

"Go on," the Chaplain said, "What does the Bible say about what happens when you die?"

The sarcastic patient's question is an authentic and important question that needs to be answered by every pastoral caregiver opening a patient's or resident's room door and being asked: "So, what are you doing here?"

What is the pastoral caregiver's role, especially in the health-care setting? According to Dr. Kenneth Doka, professor of gerontology at the Graduate School of the College of New Rochelle and senior consultant to the Hospice Foundation of America,

> *The role of a caregiver might be compared to a candle. A candle can help illuminate an experience, provide a path in the darkness and give courage to explore. The light can accompany individuals as they negotiate a sometimes*

scary and treacherous path. The journey may still be dark,
but the light can make it less terrifying.[2]

While enlightening the situation, the pastoral caregiver is
between two worlds. The pastoral caregiver who is an ordained
minister has specialized training as a Pastor in the context of a
local church. The Pastor becomes a visitor at the bedside and is
thrust into a foreign, highly specialized field with a distinct vocab-
ulary and unique set of problems. According to Lawrence Holt:

The Chaplain identifies with both worlds, yet does not feel
entirely at home in either. Chaplains are an enigma to
both worlds: medicine does not consider them 'medical
enough' and questions their relevance; the church often
does not consider them 'pastoral enough' and questions
their identity. But the fact is that despite the tensions and
enigmas, the hospital Chaplain is very much committed to
both worlds and is a vital link between them.[3]

So where can the pastoral caregiver go for help in understanding his or her role?

Frederick Greeves, an eminent British pastoral theologian,
visited the United States in the late 1950s and remarked that
"ministers 'are primarily consulted as psychologists' rather than
as pastors."[4] This observation is understandable if Greeves came
into contact with people like Carroll Wise, a prominent member
of the Rogerian school of pastoral care. Carroll Wise, author of
Pastoral Psychotherapy, taught that "We ministers do not solve
anybody's problems. . . . We are simply a means by which a person
is enabled to work out his own destiny."[5]

According to Pastor Milton, the psychological-therapeutic
movement in the modern pastoral care school, if it has been
integrated as a normative approach to pastoral care, has been a
chief contributor to an errant answer to the pressing question: "So,
what are you doing here?" Their answer might be, "I am here only
to listen." Or, if the pastoral caregiver is willing to stretch the
Rogerian model a bit: "I am here to help you get in touch with
yourself before this operation."[6]

At the very minimum, this is a departure from the normative answers that would have been provided by Pastors of the soul prior to the modern pastoral care movement. The pastoral care ministry of the Pastor is grounded in trustworthy biblical instruction, including some faithful metaphors. When these metaphors are abandoned, the effect is not only to confuse the biblical identity of the pastoral caregiver, but to also compromise, if not sacrifice, divinely attached blessings. What are some of those images that are poor options for a pastoral caregiver to portray when coming alongside people?

Inappropriate Pastoral Identities

There are some wrong identities assumed by mistaken pastoral caregivers that, if left uncorrected in one's ministry, will fail to produce comfort and cure for the patient or resident. Here are some of the default settings that some pastoral caregivers might have in their minds concerning their role in visiting the sick and dying.[7]

Therapist

With the influence of the modern pastoral care movement, as evidenced in the focus of some chaplaincy training, it's easy to understand a tendency to assume the role of a *therapist* as some go into a patient's or resident's room. With this in mind, Ralph Turnbull made this comment:

> *Some pastors fear that greater emphasis on psychology will lead to confusion by eliminating theology as the basis for the pastoral ministry. The pastor must always remember that the nature of his work as comforter is defined by the basic concept of the Christian gospel rather than by modern psychology.*[8]

One problem with the pastoral caregiver taking on the role of a therapist is that it has the potential of competing with other care-giving professionals. As such,

> *His "ministry," if that is an appropriate term, has been rerouted from prophet-priest-pastor, ambassador of Jesus Christ, to dispenser of psychological techniques whose traditions are shallow in terms of history and public recognition.*[9]

Here is an incident, as told by Michael Milton,[10] which happened in a cardiac ward of a large hospital. The patient said the hospital Chaplain came into the room, did not offer to pray or read Scripture, but conducted the visit as follows:

> *Chaplain: "So, how do you feel about being here?"*
> *Patient: "I am ready to go home, I guess. But, I know my old ticker needs a little repair, so I'm just trusting in the Lord."*
> *Chaplain: "So, you're feeling isolated."*
> *Patient: "Actually, my wife comes and goes. I think I'm fine."*
> *Chaplain: "How do you feel about being out of control at this time in your life?"*

The Chaplain, using Rogerian therapeutic techniques, was probably attempting to connect with the patient in hope of helping the patient get in touch with his feelings. Admittedly, this is a commendable endeavor. It's an attempt to show empathy in a visit. However, in the case of Christians, this approach may be entirely inadequate. They tend to expect pastoral care, not therapy. They want a pastoral caregiver to speak comforting words from Scripture, to ask about the work of the Spirit in the client's soul, and to maybe lead the client in prayer before the throne of grace.

Medical Expert

In training pastoral caregivers in clinical settings, sometimes it is observed that they have a tendency to spend too much time asking about a patient's ills and commenting on the medical treatments, as if the pastoral caregiver is a *medical expert*. Pastoral caregivers are encouraged to become familiar with medical terminology so we can better understand and speak the language of the other healthcare providers.[11] But no, we are not encouraged to use that knowledge to give medical counsel. That is not our role as a pastoral caregiver.

By way of example, consider the following pastoral visit[12]:

> *Chaplain: "How are you doing?"*
> *Patient: "They have me hooked up to all these tubes and contraptions. I'm not sure what they are or what's going on."*
> *[At this point the Chaplain could empathize with the patient over the frustration and anxiety in not under-standing what is going on, or the Chaplain could discuss the need to surrender to God in times like this, or to thank God for the blessings we don't understand. Another option is for the Chaplain to take on the role of a medical expert, as in the following comment.]*
> *Chaplain: "Well, let me see. I've been around the hospital setting for many years. It appears to me. . . ."*

One problem with assuming such a role is that it borders on professional misconduct. Such conduct is resented by the real medical professionals. Another problem with this inappropriate identity is that it confuses our role for the patient or resident. They may be puzzled as to our real purpose for being there. As a result, we may sacrifice valuable pastoral opportunities to present the Gospel, apply the Gospel, and bring the healing that only the Gospel can appropriate in their lives.

Clown

Yes, we are to "rejoice with those who rejoice," but that doesn't mean we're to act like a comedian during the visit. The clerical *clown* innocently disgraces the identity of the pastoral caregiver and confuses the role of the pastoral caregiver in visiting the sick and dying by assuming that the Chaplain is basically "a golden beam of God's sunshine for the sick."[13] Such an approach to healthcare visitation might go something like this:

Chaplain: "What a beautiful day it is outside today!"
[The patient is preparing for surgery.]
Patient: "I wouldn't know, Chaplain. I'm stuck in here."
Chaplain: "Well, it won't be long before you're able to get
outside and enjoy God's blessed creation!"

The happy clown pastoral caregiver may be using this inappropriate demeanor to hide the fact that s/he has nothing to say or doesn't know how to deal with the situation. This approach tends to minimize and ignore the real pain that people are experiencing in the midst of their ordeal.

We don't need to be "sad sacks," but we also don't need to be "jokers." Humor can be a welcome relief to a weary soul. As Katie Maxwell points out, "Encouraging someone with humor is more like subtle permission to laugh at life even in the most tense times."[14] We need to find that balance between laughter that fits the moment and that which borders on acting like a comedian. This is one reason pastoral caregivers need to engage in a training program: to learn pastoral care skills that do not use humor in an inappropriate manner.

Moral Lecturer

This inappropriate identity is usually somber and solemn, and approaches the visit with a seriousness that tries to appear worthy of the circumstances. There may be great preparation for the visit and assessment of what might ail one's soul. The problem comes by failing the test of exercising biblical wisdom as well as the wise and practical traditions of pastoral care.

The *moral lecturer* enters the patient's or resident's room, not with the theme of a servant, but as "a flint-faced, stern preacher who is intent on doing battle with the devil in the bed."[15] The pastoral caregiver's tone may sound like that of a concerned parent dealing with a wayward child. The pastoral caregiver's entire time with the client may be spent in giving advice—in trying to quickly fix the problem.

But, according to Patrick Fairbairn,

A single verse or brief passage of Scripture, uttered in a serious, affectionate, and believing manner; or the same in a few appropriate sentences, explained and applied, will often do more than a multitude of words.[16]

He goes on to say,

[Getting to the heart] will be most readily gained, not by lengthened address, or by long prayers; but by tenderness in spirit, sympathetic feeling, discriminating fidelity; faith mingling with all, and giving point and impressiveness to the sayings it brings forth from the oracles of God.[17]

Shaman

The *Shaman* is the pastoral caregiver who enters the patient's or resident's room with religious incantations and items in the hope of ridding the person and the body of evil through the use of such religious tools. In some charismatic traditions this may involve the naming of demons and the laying on of hands[18] to free the person of them. Or the Shaman may be a pastoral caregiver of a sacramental tradition where ritual is dispensed without the benefit of the Word of God to the specific situation. They often claim James 5:13-16 as their model for ministry.

Appropriate Pastoral Identities

That's enough talk about inappropriate identities for pastoral caregivers. There are some biblically faithful identities for conducting the work of visiting the sick and dying. If one rejects the modern pastoral care movement as a candidate for a biblical model, then where does one turn? After rejecting psychological identities for biblically faithful metaphors, there remain three primary models: *ambassador* (2 Corinthians 5:20), *neighbor* (Luke 10:30-37), and *comforter* (2 Corinthians 1:3-7).

Ambassador

In 2 Corinthians 5:20, Paul writes that we are an "ambassador for Christ." What does it mean to be an ambassador? An ambassador is one who speaks on the behalf of the sovereign who sent him/her. It is the duty of the ambassador to faithfully and accurately proclaim the message that was entrusted to him/her by the sovereign. In a real sense, therefore, it can be said that the message of the ambassador is the message of the sovereign—a "Word from another World."[19]

The Apostle Paul goes on to say: "We are ambassadors for Christ *as though God were pleading through us. . ."* (emphasis added). That means that wherever we go, everything we do or say will be "as though God were entreating through us." As one person put it, we may be the only "Living Bible" anyone will ever read.

That is a sobering thought. As a Pastoral Caregiver-Ambassador for Jesus Christ enters the healthcare environment, his/her role as ambassador does not automatically go on hold or into remission because s/he has entered a secular institution. The ambassador for Jesus Christ is an ambassador no matter where s/he happens to be at the moment. Ambassadors never really go on vacation. They are always hard at work, servants of their King "twenty-four/seven," as they say. This insight should deeply influence our thinking and behavior as a pastoral caregiver.

The ambassador for Jesus Christ, through his/her words and actions, is a representative of Jesus Christ. Often the sufferer is looking for a word from God and is trying to make some sense out of his/her pain and is waiting for God's ambassador to help.

An effective ambassador must have three essential skills to help meet this need. First, an ambassador must have some basic *knowledge* (an accurate *mind*). Minimally, an ambassador must know the fundamental character, mind, and purposes of the King for whom s/he serves. Second, this knowledge must be deployed in a skillful way. There is a tactful and artful diplomacy that makes our (His) message persuasive. This is called *wisdom* (an artful *method*). And third, because an ambassador brings himself/herself along in everything that is done, s/he must have good *character* (an attractive *manner*). Our personal maturity and individual virtues will either make or break our message. These three indispensable skills combine to make us a high impact representative for the Lord Jesus Christ in the healthcare setting or wherever we minsiter.

According to Proverbs 13:17, "A wicked messenger falls into trouble, but a faithful ambassador brings health." The pastoral caregiver, as an ambassador for the Great Physician of the soul, is in the patient's or resident's room to bring wellness (wholeness) in a spiritual and redemptive way that the physician of the body does not usually address.

Neighbor

The second role that Scripture mentions explicitly in relation to suffering is the role of demonstrating compassion and mercy. The parable of the Good Samaritan provides a basis for a theology of love and compassion for the hurting. In response to the question, "Who is my neighbor?" Jesus responds with the account of the Good Samaritan in Luke 10:30-37 —

Then Jesus answered and said: "A certain man went down from Jerusalem to Jericho, and fell among thieves, who stripped him of his clothing, wounded him, and departed, leaving him half dead. Now by chance a certain priest came down that road. And when he saw him, he passed by on the other side. Likewise a Levite, when he arrived at the place, came and looked, and passed by on the other side. But a certain Samaritan, as he journeyed, came where he was. And when he saw him, he had compassion. So he went to him and bandaged his wounds, pouring on oil and wine; and he set him on his own animal, brought him to an inn, and took care of him. On the next day, when he departed, he took out two denarii, gave them to the innkeeper, and said to him, 'Take care of him; and whatever more you spend, when I come again, I will repay you.' So which of these three do you think was neighbor to him who fell among the thieves?" And he said, "He who

*showed mercy on him." Then Jesus said to him, "Go and
do likewise."*

On the surface level, Jesus is teaching that any Christian, like
the Samaritan, should help others in need. However, in light of
the context of the rejection of Jesus, this parable can be seen as
a reflection of the ministry of Jesus. Jesus, like the Samaritan,
was the outcast One, who was willing to seek and save people
who were perishing. Whether one looks at the surface or views
the passage as a reflection of Jesus' ministry, the message remains:
We are to "go and do likewise," as it says in verse 37.

What does it mean to behave like a neighbor? What are we
to do? Two items are mentioned in this passage. We are to have
compassion (v. 33) and to show *mercy* (v. 37).

The parable first mentions that the Good Samaritan *"felt compassion"* (v. 33). Jesus felt compassion on numerous occasions in
His ministry (Matthew 14:14; 15:32; Mark 1:41). Scripture also
notes that Jesus often felt compassion for the lost sheep (Matthew
9:36; Mark 6:34). The term compassion is also used in Scripture
to describe the emotions of the Father as He deals with His children (Psalm 103:13-14; Luke 15:20). Indeed, the Lord is full of
compassion (Psalm 116:5)!

In the Old Testament, *hāmal* is translated "to have pity" or "to
have compassion." The Hebrew word indicates "that emotional
response which results (or may result) in action to remove its
object. . .from impending difficulty."[20] And God deeply cares
about us. The Hebrew word *rāham* means: "to love deeply" and
thus "to be compassionate."

In the New Testament, the Greek word *splanchnizomai* originally indicated the inner parts of the body and came to suggest
the seat of emotions—particularly emotions of pity, compassion,
and love. This is the word used in the Gospels to speak of Jesus
having compassion on someone in need. And in comment on the
New Testament examples of compassion, Lawrence Richards
says, "The loving compassion of one person can literally change
the life of another, for the person who cared was moved to act and
so set the needy person on a new course in life."[21]

For the believer, putting on compassion, or having compassion for one another, is a command. Colossians 3:12 reads, ". . .put on a heart of compassion." The believer is to exhibit the same heart of compassion to the suffering and the lost that Jesus exhibited in His life-changing ministry.

To feel compassion will be evidenced by pity, sympathy, understanding, patience, sensitivity, and love to those who are sick or suffering. Compassion is defined by Webster's Dictionary as sympathetic consciousness of others' distress together with a desire to alleviate it. The Good Samaritan felt compassion for the man along the road and, therefore, he responded with appropriate caregiving. We, as believers and pastoral caregivers, are to do the same.

The second thing that the Good Samaritan did was to "*show mercy*" (verse 37). Even though different words in the original languages may be found where English versions translate "mercy," the underlying concept shines through. Mercy is active love, reaching out to meet a need without considering the merit of the person who receives the aid. To show mercy means to give of oneself willingly and cheerfully. The Good Samaritan gave of his time, energy and resources to help someone in need.

The Greek verb "to show mercy" is *eleeō*. According to Lawrence Richards,

> *Originally, this word expressed only the emotion that was aroused by contact with a person who was suffering. By New Testament times, however, the concept incorporated compassionate response. A person who felt for and with a sufferer would be moved to help.*[22]

Mercy is compassionate treatment of the unfortunate in order to meet their need. And because in mercy God has brought us to life and wholeness in Jesus, showing mercy to those around us is also to be a part of our life. Our own compassion is a witness to the loving mercy of God.

Who is our neighbor? Our neighbor is anyone who is in need, and whose need we are able to meet. And while we may not always be able to explicitly define who our neighbor is, we certainly can be a good neighbor. A person should be a neighbor to anyone that s/he meets who is in need, and that includes all those who are patients in a hospital or residents in a long-term care facility or dying folks in hospice care.

It should be noted that showing mercy is mentioned as a gift of the Spirit in Romans 12:8. This does not mean that only those who have the gift of mercy are to be involved in pastoral care. Everyone who has been transformed by the compassionate mercy of God is to be involved in this ministry. However, some will show an exceptional ability in this area and will see an abundance of fruit as a result. Even though I am a Chaplain, I do not claim to have the spiritual gift of showing mercy. But God still uses me to show His mercy through me to others as I abide in Him and reach out as a loving neighbor to those in need.

Comforter

The third role that Scripture mentions explicitly in relation to coming alongside the suffering is the role of comforter. Paul writes in 2 Corinthians 1:3-7,

Blessed be the God and Father of our Lord Jesus Christ, the Father of mercies and God of all comfort, who comforts us in all our tribulation, that we may be able to comfort those who are in any trouble, with the comfort with which we ourselves are comforted by God. But if anyone has caused grief, he has not grieved me, but all of you to some extent—not to be too severe. This punishment which was inflicted by the majority is sufficient for such a man, so that, on the contrary, you ought rather to forgive and comfort him, lest perhaps such a one be swallowed up with too much sorrow.

All Christians experience afflictions. And probably no one experienced any more afflictions as a Christian than Paul. He was beaten, stoned, shipwrecked, robbed, hungry, and weak. Through all of this, Paul encourages Christians to shift their perspective from the temporal hassles to the eternal hope. Christians are to keep their eyes focused on Jesus Christ and not focused upon the temporal sufferings that might steal their attention away from the Lord.

The source of all comfort in the midst of our afflictions is God Himself. He is the God of all comfort. Comfort that is received from God enables believers to comfort others. The comfort of God is channeled through His people to help others in the midst of their afflictions.

Two questions probably need to be raised in order to properly evaluate the pastoral caregiver's role as it relates to this aspect of a ministry of comfort. First, is this affliction only referring to and applicable to outside pressures and not to personal, physical affliction? Second, what does it mean to comfort one another?

While it is true that the Corinthian church was experiencing a great deal of outside pressure, it does not appear that the context of this passage can be limited only to outside pressure. In verse 4, when Paul speaks of afflictions (*thlipsei*), he is referring to any kind of pressure or helpless distress. When the word is used in the verse with the article, it means: "all the tribulation actually encountered." When the word is used without the article, as in this verse, it means "any kind of affliction." In other words, with the article the words mean "the whole of" the affliction; without the article, as in this text, it means "every kind of" affliction.

God comforts us constantly and unfailingly, not intermittently. And He does so in all of our afflictions, not merely in certain kinds of suffering. For us as a believer, then, our ministry should be in line with the ministry of God. We should comfort and encourage others in whatever affliction they may be suffering.

So, what does it mean to comfort someone? The word comfort means to impart strength and hope. It includes the concept of soothing distress or depression. The word that is used here is from the Greek word *paraclēsis*. This is the same word used to describe the ministry of the Holy Spirit. It describes, in the basic sense, an advocate who stands beside a person to encourage him/her when that person is undergoing severe testing. The Holy Spirit, as our "Paraclete" (John 14:16; 15:26), comes alongside us to strengthen and guide us, to comfort and console us. Likewise, our ministry to others who are suffering should be one of standing beside them, comforting and encouraging them during their time of need.

Scripture does provide these three models of ministry to the suffering: ambassador, neighbor, and comforter. The main characteristics that can be isolated from these three models include: one who is a witness for Christ, has a compassionate heart and shows mercy, and is a comforter who stands beside the person to encourage him/her during times of need. These characteristics make up the primary roles of a pastoral caregiver as ambassador, neighbor and comforter.

The Use of Scripture and Prayer in Visitation

The Scriptures offer a stability and hope to which both we and those we visit can turn. In a changing, fragmented and chaotic world, the Word of God directs our attention to a perfect God who never changes and who can put order and meaning into our afflicted lives.

The spiritual resources of Scripture and prayer are best utilized in the context of a visit during which some kind of rapport has been established with the patient or resident through the pastoral caregiver's presence and attentive listening. One of the common tendencies, especially when someone is new to visitation, is to rush too quickly to use Scripture and/or prayer without taking time to listen and establish a pastoral presence with the person. Hasty advice (unwelcome "preaching") that tries to offer a quick fix to the problem (often through the misuse of these resources) is not good pastoral care. The Dutch Christian writer, Henri Nouwen, once said,

> *When we honestly ask ourselves which person in our lives mean the most to us, we often find that it is those who, instead of giving advice, solutions, or cures, have chosen rather to share our pain and touch our wounds with a warm and tender hand. The friend who can be silent with us in a moment of despair or confusion, who can stay with us in an hour of grief and bereavement, who can tolerate*

not knowing, not curing, not healing and face with us the reality of our powerlessness, that is a friend who cares.[23]

So, use Scripture and prayer appropriately. This means we first take time to listen to them tell their story so we can identify their spiritual needs and know that the verse we finally share with them relates specifically to their situation. In addition, it means that we have received their permission (informed consent) to share a verse from the Bible and apply it to their life. Nothing is more helpful to the sick and suffering than to hear what God's Word has to say to them and their particular situation. And nothing is more unsupportive than when Scripture is inappropriately imposed on those who are hurting.

Sharing Scripture

The following are some helpful hints in the use of Scripture.

Find an appropriate time. Referring to Scripture too soon can give the impression the Bible has only pat (and therefore trite) answers. Referring to it too late makes it seem like an afterthought. "A person finds joy in giving an apt reply—and how good is a timely word!" (Proverbs 15:23, NIV). We first of all need to be sure that we really understand the situation and then we share the right Scripture verse at the appropriate time.

Choose the appropriate verse. Our choice should be guided by the person's needs rather than our agenda. We need to give ourselves time to find out their needs as we listen to their story.

Choose the appropriate translation. Many elderly, who are versed in the Bible, are familiar with the King James Bible and will expect us to read this version. For those who are unfamiliar with the Bible, consider using a modern version—one that they can read and understand with ease (such as the NLT). Having a Bible app on our phone makes using different translations a fairly simple task.

If we already know the situation before the visit, we may pre-decide on an appropriate passage of encouragement. Be careful, though, for we may be putting our own agenda forward, ahead of the patient's or resident's perceived spiritual needs.

If we have had permission to read (or quote) a verse to the patient or resident, we may want to leave the verse with them (for example, before they go into surgery). We can write it on our business card or a "post it" note.

If there is a Bible in the room, read from it.

Do not overwhelm the patient or resident with a lot of verses. One will usually do. Some folks won't have the stamina to listen to a long reading, so be sensitive and focus on one verse and its plain meaning.

Keep it in mind that if the person has a problem, we need to let them wrestle with the Word of God and not with us.

Remember to always obtain permission (informed consent) before reading from the Bible or leaving a verse (or literature) with the patient or resident. The person may see Scripture as intrusive or even as proselytizing. We need to be sensitive to the person's receptivity to having a verse shared with them when we attempt to share Scripture.

Remember Job's "comforters"? Don't be accused of being a miserable comforter because of shoving a verse down their throat (Job 16:2).

Scripture for Specific Situations

Here are some verses that may be used in particular situations, if appropriate to share:

- For those in need of **Comfort**: Psalm 23; 103:1-14; 2 Corinthians 1:3-5.
- For those **Facing Surgery**: Deuteronomy 31:8; 33:27; Isaiah 41:10; Psalm 34; 46; 91; 121. Note: We may want to avoid using Psalm 23 (unless specifically requested by the patient or resident) since it is often associated with death and dying (like at funerals).
- For those who are **Recovering from Surgery**: Psalm 34; 1 Peter 5:5-7, 10.
- For those in need of **Guidance and Wisdom**: Psalm 32:8; Proverbs 3:5-6; James 1:5-6.
- For those who are fearful, anxious, or nervous:

Fear: Deuteronomy 31:8; Psalm 23:4; 27:1; 34:4; 121:1-8; Isaiah 41:10; Matthew 10:28; Luke 12:5; Romans 8:15; 2 Timothy 1:7; 1 John 4:18.

Anxiety (Worry): Isaiah 26:3; Psalm 16:11; 37:1, 7; 107; Proverbs 12:25; 16:7; Matthew 6:19-34; Philippians 4:6-7, 19; 1 Peter 5:6-7.

Nervous: Nahum 1:7.

- For comfort in times of darkness:

  Death: Psalm 23; 116:15; 130; Proverbs 14:32; John 14:1-4; 11:25-26; 1 Corinthians 15:54-58; 2 Corinthians 5:6-8; Philippians 1:21-23; Hebrews 2:14-15.

  Depression (feeling **downhearted**): Psalm 27; 34; 38; 42:5-11; Proverbs 18:14; Isaiah 40:28-31; 1 Corinthians 15:58; 2 Corinthians 4:8-18.

  Discouragement: Psalm 23; 55:22; Matthew 5:11-12; 2 Corinthians 4:8-18.

- For those going through **Pain and Suffering**: Job 5:17-18; Psalm 38; 41:1-3; Matthew 26:39; John 16:33; James 5:14-15; 2 Corinthians 1:3-5; 12:7-10; 1 Peter 1:3-7; 4:12-13, 19.

- For those needing **Forgiveness**: Psalm 32:1-7; 51; 103:1-5; Isaiah 1:18; Colossians 2:11-15; 1 John 1:6-9.

- For those who feel **Guilty**: Psalm 32:1-5; John 8:36; Romans 7:18-25; 8:1; Philippians 3:13-14.

- For the **Birth of a Baby**: Psalm 127; 139; Mark 10:13-16; Luke 1:14.

- For the **Death of a Baby**: Psalm 139; Isaiah 7:15; 2 Samuel 12:23.

- For those who are **Weary** and in need of **Rest and Refreshment**: Psalm 4:7-8; 90; Jeremiah 6:16; Matthew 11:28-30; John 4:7-10; 10:10; 14:27; Galatians 6:9-10.

- For those who are in need of **Hope**: Psalm 71:5-6; Lamentations 3:1-24; Romans 5:2-5; 12:12; 1 Peter 1:3.

- For those who feel **Lonely**: Exodus 33:14; Psalm 91:11; Isaiah 41:10; Matthew 28:18-20; Hebrews 13:5-6.

- For those in need of **Peace**: Isaiah 26:3; Romans 8:6; Philippians 4:6-7; Colossians 3:15.

- For those in need of **Strength and Courage**: Joshua 1:7-9; 2 Corinthians 12:9.

Praying with People

Why should we pray with clients? Here are a few reasons prayer might be needed and helpful:

- To direct them toward God—the source of healing (wellness, wholeness).
- To encourage them emotionally and spiritually.
- To offer the grace and peace of Christ.
- To acknowledge dependence on the Father.
- To lift up (share) a common concern (burden).

When should we pray with clients? Here are some timing issues related to praying with clients:

- After we have identified the needs to be met (through listening to them). It is important not to pray with someone before adequate communication has taken place. Then the prayer can reflect to God the personal concerns that have come out of the conversation.
- When we sense the proper context exists. Sometimes prayer needs to come near the beginning of the visit, and other times it is needed in the middle or end of the visit. There are some situations when our presence is enough and prayer is not needed.
- When we sense that the ministry of prayer would be appreciated by them (for example, they actually ask us to pray for them).
- After we have asked for permission to pray. Realize that some may see prayer as intrusive. So be sensitive when attempting to pray with a client.

When should we *not* pray with clients? Here are some situations when prayer should not be used:

- If we do not have their permission to pray with them, we do not pray.
- If we are using prayer as some type of supernatural potion or magic wand, as a judgmental statement, or as a superficial ritual lacking sincerity, then don't pray.
- If we are using prayer as a means to gain merit with God, then we should be quiet.

How should we pray with clients? Prayer is a pastoral care tool that needs to be used with care. Here are some guidelines for praying with the sick and suffering:

- First listen. Listen for their needs (spoken and unspoken). Then contextualize the prayer—bringing in topics or concerns that were discussed in the conversation and feelings that were expressed. Discern their hopes, fears and desires, and then take them before the throne of grace.
- Be open for the right moment, the right timing. Sometimes we can only capture that moment non-verbally. Always ask permission to pray with a client. We need to trust ourselves to be God's agent for that specific moment.
- Be as specific as possible. Pray for their particular needs they brought up during the conversation.
- Be brief. Stay with the attention span of the client. Keep in mind that sick hospital patients are often in pain or discomfort and have a short attention span. This is not a time for a mini-sermon in our prayer.
- Adjust to the person's background. Tailor the prayer to the person's faith tradition. For example, with Muslims I pray to Almighty God (not "Our Father," which would be offensive to them). In addition, don't end the prayer "in Jesus' name" with Muslim or Jewish clients. Simply say "Amen" or "In the name of Him who is ever gracious and merciful."
- Focus on God. Praise God for who He is (especially His love and compassion) and what He has done (highlight personal situations the person has mentioned). Pray with

a heart of thanksgiving for the grace of God in the midst of the ordeal.

- Personalize the prayer. Use the person's name. Use their first name only with their permission to do so; otherwise, use their last name.
- Involve the client in the prayer, if possible. Ask if they would like to pray, but don't pressure them.
- Use "we" statements only when we think/feel the person would join us in the sentiment. Otherwise, use mostly "I" statements. That way if we prayed something the client doesn't agree with, s/he will not feel coerced or trapped in the prayer.
- Include others who may be present. Some Chaplains have them all hold hands as they pray together (again, ask for permission to do this).
- Pray with hope. This is not wishing for better circumstances. It is encouraging hope for a vision of believing God for a future with real possibilities.
- If it fits with their religious tradition, we may want to offer the Lord's Prayer and invite them to join in praying this with you.
- We may wish to extend some expression of a sincere blessing (and this may be our only "prayer" with and for the person). This can be as simple as saying, "God be with you," or "May God bless you." It can be very meaningful for a client to hear a blessing from someone who truly cares. For example,
  The LORD bless you and keep you; The LORD make His face shine upon you, and be gracious to you; The LORD lift up His countenance upon you, and give you peace (Numbers 6:24-26).
- Don't pray and run. Prayer might release more emotions and further conversation. If we see tears after the prayer, we might ask, "This seems to have touched something in you. Do you want to talk about it?"

In conclusion on this subject of prayer at the bedside, Chaplain Kirkwood says it "requires a developing sensitivity to where a patient is, a deepening intimacy between you and your God and a growing ability to utilize these in tandem."[24]

Literature

Importance. One of the most appreciated aspects of the pastoral caregiver's ministry may be the literature that s/he gives to clients. Most patients or residents will gladly accept something to read, especially if it is on good paper with a nice picture on the cover. One prison patient read the entire Bible while he was in the security ward of the hospital. Many have found hope and encouragement from things that the pastoral caregiver has given to them. Some may not want to discuss spiritual issues, but they will read Christian literature given to them. Even so, some people will perceive literature as intrusive (and maybe even as proselytizing). So, be sensitive when attempting to give out literature. Only give it with their permission ("informed consent").

Policy. The Chaplain at the facility is in charge of all distribution of religious literature in the healthcare facility. It is best to only place literature in waiting rooms after obtaining permission from the Chaplain's Office. The Chaplain at the hospital will regularly remove from public areas literature that is from a particular church or religious group. Policies tend to vary greatly from one healthcare organization to another. Some may not allow religious literature of any kind in the waiting rooms.

Generally, it is best to have a few pieces of literature with which we are familiar that can be used, rather than to use whatever people wish to donate for us to use. It is also best not to use theologically "heavy" or lengthy material because of the religious diversity and physical condition of many patients and residents we will visit.

Bibles

A Gideon representative will provide New Testaments with the Psalms to give to patients or residents and whole Bibles to place in waiting rooms. Because of a concern for the spread of contagious diseases from one patient to another, many hospitals do not allow these Bibles to remain at the bedside after a patient is discharged. In such cases, Bibles are only given out when a patient requests one. New Testaments in large print, various languages and modern translations can be ordered at a subsidized price from the American Bible Society and kept in the Chaplain's Office or Chapel. NIV copies of the Gospel of John in English and Spanish can be purchased from the International Bible Society.

Tracts

Although tracts are often refused outside the healthcare institution, some patients and residents will ask for them. Excellent tracts presenting the Gospel and offering comfort and hope are available from Good News Publishers and the American Tract Society. The latter also has cartoon tracts for young people.

The best tracts are those that we write ourselves. We could write one with our own testimony or the testimonies of others. Many churches will print these and other leaflets for the pastoral caregiver. Some people are interested in giving to projects and will donate funds for such literature who would otherwise not contribute to the support of a pastoral care program.

Periodicals

Probably the favorites of most patients and residents (and staff) are *Guideposts* and *Our Daily Bread*. These may be received free in quantity for distribution. Another free periodical you may want to consider for sharing is the *Decision* magazine.

Booklets

The Bible League has some excellent booklets, such as *Someone Cares, God Understands, Who Cares When I Hurt,* and *Answers to Live By.* One very good mini booklet is the *Gos-pill*, which can be purchased from S-O-S Publishers. CareNotes from Abbey Press bring messages of hope and comfort to those in need. They are in an easy-to-read and non-imposing format. They cover such topics as grief and loss, personal healing and growth, elder care and spiritual care. PrayerNotes from Abbey Press are said to "bring prayer to people—and bring people to prayer." They also celebrate special religious occasions like Advent and Lent.

Leaflets

Scripture verses, helpful readings and word puzzles on a one-page format can be printed up by your church. We might also wish to produce a leaflet informing people of pastoral care services that can be placed in the foyer of the church or handed out during a worship service.

Letters

Some pastoral caregivers send bereavement follow up letters to the next of kin of those who have died. Some also send personal congratulation letters to mothers who have had a baby born in the hospital.

Literature

Listed below are several organizations that provide written tools that may be used in ministering to clients.
American Bible Society (www.americanbible.org)
American Tract Society (www.atstracts.org)
Bible League Int'l (www.bibleleagueusa.com)
CareNotes / PrayerNotes (www.onecaringplace.com)
Decision Magazine (www.billygraham.org)
Good News / Crossway (www.gnpcb.org)
Guideposts (www.guideposts.com)
International Bible Society (www.ibs.org)
Our Daily Bread (www.gospelcom.net)
RBC Ministries (www.rbc.org)

Communion

The pastoral caregiver may want to have a small communion set (with disposable cups) for patients or residents who occasionally request the Lord's Supper. We can also contact our Pastor to come in and offer communion to the person.

Before giving anything by mouth, we must first check with the nurse to make sure that there are no medical conditions that would not permit the patient to take anything by mouth.

Questions for Review

1. Can you give a description of at least one inappropriate pastoral identity?
2. How would you describe the qualities of one of the appropriate pastoral identities?
3. Can you explain a situation when it's probably not okay to share a Scripture verse with someone?
4. When might you want to pray with someone?

Questions for Reflection

1. Take time to reflect on Luke 6:41-42. Write a reflection on how this applies to you and your role as a pastoral caregiver (describe the "splinters/logs" in your life). Explain how you might tend to be (or not be) a self-aware person who judges, assesses, and knows yourself. In what areas of pastoral care might you tend to be a hypocrite? Record your insights in a journal and discuss them with a confidant and/or the training team.
2. Write down and memorize at least one Bible verse for fear, one verse for those entering surgery, and one verse to comfort those dealing with death. Share and discuss the appropriate use of these Bible verses with your training team.
3. As you think about families experiencing prolonged illness, list five possible scenarios, and write down resources that could be of assistance in ministering to these families

in each of the potential scenarios. Share and discuss the appropriate use of these resources with your training team.

Chapter Resources

Becker, Arthur H. *The Compassionate Visitor: Resources for Ministering to People Who Are Ill.* Minneapolis, MN: Augsburg, 1985.

Cabot, Richard C., and Russell L. Dicks. *The Art of Ministering to the Sick.* New York: Macmillan, 1936.

Chapin, Shelley. *Counselors, Comforters, and Friends.* Wheaton, IL: Victor, 1992.

Clinebell, Howard, Howard W. Stone, and William M. Clements. *Basic Types of Pastoral Care & Counseling. Resources for the Ministry of Healing and Growth.* Nashville: Abingdon, 1987.

Collins, Gary R. *How to Be a People Helper.* Wheaton, IL: Tyndale House Pub., 1995.

Dyksra, Robert C., ed. *Images of Pastoral Care: Classic Readings.* St. Louis: Chalice, 2005.

Eyer, Richard C. *Pastoral Care Under the Cross: God in the Midst of Suffering.* St. Louis: Concordia Pub. House, 1994.

Faber, Heije. *Pastoral Care in the Modern Hospital.* Philadelphia: Westminster, 1971.

Hansen, David. *The Art of Pastoring: Ministry without All the Answers.* Downers Grove, IL: InterVarsity, 1994.

Haugk, Kenneth C. *Christian Caregiving: A Way of Life.* Minneapolis, MN: Augsburg, 1984.

Heuch, Johan, and J. Melvin Moe *Pastoral Care of the Sick.* Minneapolis, MN: Augsburg, 1949.

Hunter, Rodney J. *Dictionary of Pastoral Care and Counseling.* Nashville: Abingdon, 1990.

King, Diana. *Faith, Spirituality and Medicine: Toward the Making of the Healing Practitioner.* New York: Haworth Pastoral, 2000.

Lauterbach, William Albert. *Ministering to the Sick.* St. Louis: Concordia Pub. House, 1955.

Lester, Andrew D. *Hope in Pastoral Care and Counseling.* Louisville, KY: Westminster/John Knox, 1995.

Nelson, Alan E. *Five-minute Ministry: Ten Simple Principles for You to Make a Difference*. Grand Rapids, MI: Baker, 1993.

Niklas, Gerald R., and Charlotte Stephanics. *Ministry to the Hospitalized*. New York: Paulist, 1975.

Oden, Thomas C. *Classical Pastoral Care*. Grand Rapids, MI: Baker, 2000.

Pellegrino, Edmund D., and David C. Thomasma. *Helping and Healing: Religious Commitment in Health Care*. Washington, DC: Georgetown UP, 1997.

Pennel, Joe E., Jr. *The Gift of Presence: A Guide to Helping Those Who Suffer*. Nashville, TN: Abingdon, 2009.

Pennington, Robert. *The Christ Chaplain: The Way to a Deeper, More Effective Hospital Ministry*. New York: Routledge, 2007.

Purves, Andrew. *The Search for Compassion: Spirituality and Ministry*. Louisville, KY: Westminster, 1989.

Ryan, Juanita R. *Standing By*. Wheaton, IL: Tyndale House Pub., 1984.

Shelly, Judith Allen. *Spiritual Care: A Guide for Caregivers*. Downers Grove, IL: InterVarsity, 2000.

Slater, Michael. *Stretcher Bearers: Practicing and Receiving the Gift of Encouragement and Support*. Ventura, CA: Regal, 1985.

Smith, Doug. *Being a Wounded Healer*. Madison, WI: Psycho-Spiritual Publications, 1999.

Speck, Peter. *Being There: Pastoral Care in Time of Illness*. London: SPCK, 1988.

Stevenson-Moessner, Jeanne. *A Primer in Pastoral Care*. Minneapolis: Fortress, 2005

Thompson, Chuck. *Presence and Truth*. Enumclaw, WA: Pleasant Word, 2004.

5

Coming Alongside the Dying

Somebody should tell us,
right at the start of our lives,
that we are dying.
Then we might live life to the limit,
every minute of every day.
Do it! I say.
Whatever you want to do, do it now!
There are only so many tomorrows.
— Pope Paul VI (1897-1978)

My heart is in anguish within me,
And the terrors of death have fallen upon me.
— David (Psalm 55:4, NASB)

When this happens—when our perishable earthly bodies
have been transformed into heavenly bodies that will never
die—then at last the Scriptures will come true:
"Death is swallowed up in victory.
O death, where is your victory?
O death, where is your sting?"
— Apostle Paul (1 Corinthians 15:54-55, NLT)

M ost people will choose to handle death in the same manner they choose to handle life. This has been my observation as a Chaplain and this is what I think Dr. Jim Towns, who teaches classes and lectures on the subject of death and dying, means when he says,

> *According to a person's philosophical or theological perspective, he will develop a style of living and dying. A person's style of dying is inherent in his style of living. A person's attitude about illness, dying and death depend on his systems of beliefs.*[1]

And when we, as pastoral caregivers, come alongside such people, we need to be sensitive to all of these issues. So let's talk about a ministry to those facing death.

Pre-Death Grief Response[2]

To effectively minister to the terminally ill person, it is helpful to understand the emotional process s/he might experience. When a person knows s/he is going to die, that individual usually experiences five different "stages" or seasons of emotional response.[3] You will also find that his/her loved ones often go through these same emotional reactions. However, we must keep in mind the fact that each person approaches death in a unique and individual manner. We also need to understand that these "stages" or phases are not always in a specific order or experienced by every person every time. Few dying patients or residents go through these stages as if they were climbing a ladder one rung at a time. Nevertheless, they do offer a general framework of which we should be aware.

A Season of Denial

What to Expect

The first reaction is usually an intellectual refusal to accept or believe the prognosis of his/her condition. Some people make such statements as, "It can't be! They're wrong! There must be a mistake of some kind!"

There are many forms of denial. They may go from doctor to doctor seeking another diagnosis and searching for some ray of hope. They may deny that they are ill at all. They may refuse to believe that the diagnosis is correct or reject the idea that the disease is fatal. They may pretend that the diagnosis doesn't bother them in any way and go on living as if nothing has happened. The person with a fatal illness may show his/her denial in ways other than words. S/he may make unrealistic plans, look forward to events far beyond his/her life expectancy, disobey doctor's orders, refuse to accept limitations, and/or make over-optimistic statements about the therapy.

It is also important to realize and respect the fact that a patient's or resident's state of denial can fluctuate from day to day. The reason one's denial may fluctuate is probably dictated by the degree of stress s/he is under at any given time. The amount of denial a person expresses is usually that which is required to get along comfortably. That is because denial is essentially that mechanism by which a person is enabled to put out of mind the morbid, upsetting, frightening, depressing, and pessimistic aspects of his/her life while focusing on more positive and constructive issues like the business of living.

Denial has been called the "emotional shock-absorber" to tragedy. Therefore, it is not necessarily unhealthy to experience it. It is needed as a buffer or safety zone. Through denial a person's emotions are temporarily desensitized. It allows time for a terrifying idea to "sink in" so people can "collect" themselves. Denial freezes a person's emotions for a certain amount of time before reality must be faced, but those emotions must be thawed out eventually.

Denial becomes harmful and pathological when it blocks out and prevents the grieving process altogether. Jeremiah 6:14

explains that we cannot heal a wound by saying that it is not there. If a person's denial is so distorted that a communication barrier has come between the person and the family, and s/he is becoming more and more isolated from them, then it is time to gently break through the denial so that some meaningful sharing can take place. If the person's relationships are good, and s/he is not doing anything self-destructive, then the denial really is not all that "bad." Denial should be honored as long as it is adaptive.

With regard to the value of denial, Joyce Landorf has said:

> *We need denial—but we must not linger in it. We must recognize it as one of God's most unique tools and use it. Denial is our special oxygen mask to use when the breathtaking news of death has sucked every ounce of air out of us. It facilitates our bursting lungs by giving them their first gulps of sorrow-free air. We breathe in the breath of denial and it seems to maintain life. We do not need to feel guilty or judge our level of Christianity for clutching the mask to our mouth. However, after breathing has been restored and the initial danger has passed, we need not be dependent on it.*
>
> *I think God longs for us to lay down the oxygen mask of denial, and with His help begin breathing into our lungs the fresh, free air of acceptance on our own.*[4]

Ways to Respond

Remember: This stage of skepticism may be necessary to give the patient or resident and his/her family the opportunity to gather the personal resources that will allow them to face the ultimate outcome of this serious illness—death.

We need to be tactful—gentle, yet firm. We must never contribute to the person's fantasy by giving false hope, or upset him/her by emphatically insisting that s/he is wrong. We must always be empathetic and understanding.

Do not judge the person for what is being said at this time. A simple, honest statement might be helpful, such as, "Yes, you have terminal cancer and I'm very sorry. I know it must be very hard for you to accept. But be assured that I will be here for you through the journey." Eventually the person will respond because s/he needs someone with whom to share his/her loss and loneliness.

Simply being with the person and the family is an important ministry. Never underestimate the power of our pastoral presence.

Touch is also vital because it expresses a common bond and sharing of existence. It is surely one of the most important forms of nonverbal communication with a dying person and is usually not done enough. Holding a hand while listening or praying can be a meaningful ministry of caring for the person.

Some Scripture verses we may want to share during this time are: Psalm 4; 16; 18:1-6; 23; 30; 31; 40; Romans 8; 2 Corinthians 1:3-11; Hebrews 4:14-16. Can you think of other verses that would be helpful to someone going through denial?

A Season of Anger

What to Expect
Realizing, at least in part, that s/he will die, the terminal patient or resident may openly express anger, rage, envy and/or resentment. Instead of responding with "No, not me," the person now responds with, "Yes, but why me?" The person may:

- Be angry with friends and relatives who are well.
- Complain about the medical care or gripe about the food.
- Be angry with the doctor who cannot make him/her well.
- Be angry with God for allowing this to happen and for not immediately providing healing.
- Say something like, "I didn't do anything to deserve this. It's not fair!"

In Job 7:11 it says, "Therefore I will not restrain my mouth; I will speak in the anguish of my spirit; I will complain in the bitterness of my soul." Some other examples of anger in the Bible can be found in 1 Samuel 20:30-33; Jonah 4:1; and Luke 15:28.

Ways to Respond
We should not take such anger personally. They are not angry at us, but at their situation. Nor should we become judgmental and

say that the person should not feel so angry. This is simply part of the normal process most people experience, and it usually helps them relieve the anguish of dying by being able to express it.

Active listening is very helpful in dealing with the angry person. Allow the person to verbalize the reasons for his/her anger and to vent specifically how s/he feels. The person could be merely demanding attention. Honest and open communication can help him/her feel understood as we affirm what s/he is feeling.

When dealing with a person in this stage of reaction, try to be brief and direct, avoiding anything that sounds like preaching. The person who is perceived as helpful during this time is the one who cares enough to listen and understand the other person.

Some Bible verses that may be shared during this stage are: Psalm 4:1-4; 6:1-5; 22; 31; Proverbs 15:1; Ecclesiastes 1:1-4; Matthew 5:21-22; Mark 14:32-42; Ephesians 4:26, 31; James 1:19-20. Can you think of others that might be helpful to share with an angry person?

A Season of Bargaining

What to Expect

Realizing s/he is in fact dying, the person may attempt to postpone death by offering good behavior or service as an exchange for a longer life. The dying person now pleads, "Yes, I know I'm dying, but spare me!"

This stage usually lasts only a brief period of time, but it can be intense while it lasts. The bargain usually involves a specific promise: "If I can get well then I will serve the Lord more than ever," or "I'll be satisfied if only I can live to see my grandchildren," and the list of bargains goes on and on. These bargains are usually made in secret and are often made with God. Keep in mind that family members can bargain just as much as the terminally ill person.

Part of the bargaining process could reflect their reaction to death and to God. They may feel that God simply does not know what He's doing and they need to straighten Him out. Others could be allowed to die, they reason, but in this case He's wrong. In response to such questions, Joe Bayly made this comment in his book, *The View from a Hearse*: "Death for the Christian should be a shout of triumph, through sorrow and tears, bringing glory to God—not a confused misunderstanding of the will of God to heal."[5]

Joyce Landorf shares a story of a lady and her experience with bargaining:

> *She had lost her first husband after thirty years of marriage. Two years later she had married again and had seven happy years with a second husband. Then he got cancer.*
>
> *She told me they had been so very happy and the seven years had been so short that she pleaded and bargained with God to heal her husband. He was very close to dying and she knelt by his bed and begged the Lord to heal him so he wouldn't die. She said the Lord's voice spoke so clearly that she was quite startled by it. She heard Him say very distinctly in her mind, 'Your husband has prepared himself to accept death and to die right now. Tell Me, do you want him to prepare himself for death again—later on?' She opened her eyes and looked at her husband—he was at peace—he had reached acceptance. She said, `Oh, Joyce, I knew right then I'd have to release him. At that moment a great peace settled over me. He died a few hours later. Both of us were at peace.' If she had hung on, begged God to let her husband live, she would have missed what God wanted to do in their lives.*[6]

Ways to Respond

We might review with them the story of the fiery furnace and point out the conditional clause in the statement of deliverance of the men involved (see Daniel 3:18). Another option is to look at 1 Peter 1, a chapter that deals with hope in the face of extreme difficulty. See also Psalm 39:13; 2 Kings 20:1; and Isaiah 18 for additional examples of bargaining. Can you think of other Scripture verses that would be helpful at this time?

How should we pray for a person who is bargaining? Should we pray for complete healing? Perhaps our prayer ought to be more focused on more pain-free moments for the person, for his/her more complete knowledge of God (Psalm 46:10), for the person's relationship to Christ to become stronger, and/or for his/her positive witness with the doctors, nurses, friends and relatives. Even so, it is not wrong to call upon the Lord of grace for healing (wholeness, wellness).

Our ministry at this time is to be a good listener. We need to respect the need to bargain, realizing that it is actually a part of hope. False reassurances will not be helpful. Simple reflection, a meaningful touch, and empathic listening will minister to the person struggling with the reality of facing death. Try to show them the implications of their bargaining, but do so in a loving, constructive manner. Please, no lectures or pious platitudes at this time.

A Season of Depression

What to Expect
Denial has not worked. Anger has not worked. Bargaining has not worked. Therefore, the individual facing death concludes that nothing works—and now depression tends to set in. Aware that s/he will lose all those whom s/he loves, thinking of the many things s/he will never live to see or do, and anticipating his/her steady deterioration, the terminal person may now become downhearted and withdrawn: brooding, feeling sad, and being inconsolable. The dying person now responds by saying, "Yes, it's me! What's the use? I'll never feel good again. I'm going to die!" Such feelings of despair are a normal part of preparing to die.

This depression has two parts:

One is called *reactive* depression. The person thinks about past memories (mourning for what is already lost: health, independence, mobility, uncompleted work, and an inability to meet responsibilities). Reactive depression often occurs in response to feelings of helplessness, loss of control, and lowered self-esteem associated with serious illness. This depression may also be associated with feelings of abandonment by family members and others, actual or imagined insensitivities of medical staff, and such real world issues as finances.

The second is called *preparatory* depression. The person thinks about impending losses that s/he has held dear (mourning for what is still to be lost: family, friends, and all that might have been). Preparatory depression may be evidenced by frightening dreams, irritability, sadness, anorexia, apathy, and, on occasion, suicidal preoccupations. This depression represents the dying person's mourning for self, personal relationships, and physical impotence.

Ways to Respond
This is a time when the person needs to express sorrow and to pour it out. We can minister best at this time by sitting silently with the person or holding a hand and letting him/her know that it is okay to express feelings of loss. Please do not argue or debate with him/her, for the consequences of doing this can only be negative.

The dying person may also be feeling unnecessary guilt and shame for causing sadness to family and friends, or for being a "burden" to them. Allow the person to grieve, but also help him/her to relieve the guilt, if possible.

It can be helpful to focus attention on the concrete and real-life situations causing the person difficulty, and to mobilize available support. Help facilitate communication with his/her family. If possible, help ease financial burdens (for example, by making a referral to the social worker or a financial planner). Help him/her adjust to body-image changes.

It is not helpful to interrupt the person's preparatory responses with false promises. It is important not to rush the person through this season of depression, but to help him/her gain a sense of closure through the process.

Although we cannot offer false hope at this juncture, the following Scriptures can be an encouragement: Psalm 22:1-24; 23; 31; 32; 37; 38; 42; 43:5; 51; 60; 62; 63; 142; Matthew 11:28; John 14:16-18; 16:20-22; 1 Corinthians 15; 2 Corinthians 4:8-9; Philippians 4:13. Can you think of other verses that would be helpful to someone who is downhearted?

In using God's Word, we should emphasize the faithfulness and love which God has for His children, rather than stressing what God is trying to teach him/her through this experience (even though there may be an important lesson to be learned at this time). Biblical examples of depression are found in the life of Elijah (1 Kings 19:4), David (2 Samuel 12:16-24), Job (Job 1:1; 19:25-26), and the sons of Korah (Psalm 42—43).

A Season of Acceptance

What to Expect

Acceptance is the final stage in the emotional process of dying. Having faced and struggled with the reality of his/her own death, the person now rests in the knowledge of what will happen. This is not necessarily a happy time for the person, but it is a time of emotional calm—no great fear, joy or sadness—often marked by increasing withdrawal and long periods of sleep. The dying person has given consent to death, saying, "Yes, I'm ready now." It is a healthy coming to terms with reality and allowing the world to go on without him/her. There is nothing else to do but to accept the inevitable.

Does anyone ever really accept death? For many a seriously ill person, death is a welcome visitor, especially where pain or prolonged suffering cause a person to view death as a desirable release from that suffering. Though many do make themselves ready, there are always some who seem to be caught unprepared.

Ways to Respond

The adage, "We bring to our dying the resources of our living" seems most often to be accurate. We need to respect the individual's right to complete his/her life in ways that are meaningful to him/her (which may not be so acceptable to us). Not everyone reaches the kind of acceptance about impending death that we hope they will. Knowing this can help us minimize unrealistic expectations.

The person who has come to accept his/her impending death may lose all interest in life at this point and even become less talkative. At this stage in the process of dying, the pastoral caregiver's attention often turns towards an even greater involvement with the person's family. Family members often ask, "What do I say to my loved one?" The greatest words of solace are: "I love you—regardless and always." Tell the family members to let the dying person know what s/he has meant to them. Have them be specific in their affirmations.

Phases of Dying

Dr. Pattison[7] divided the seasons, or phases, of dying into the following three categories:

The *Acute Phase*. This initial phase involves the denial, anger and bargaining already discussed.

The *Chronic Living/Dying Phase*. This phase is focused on fears: the fear of abandonment, loss of self-control, suffering and pain, loss of personal identity, the unknown, and the fear of regression into self.

The *Terminal Phase*. This phase is concerned mostly with withdrawal issues.

Tasks Related to the Phases of Dying

Using the above three phases as a guideline, there are several tasks involved in dealing with a life-threatening illness.[8] Look at each one listed below and reflect on ways we might minister to someone facing each of these tasks.

General Tasks
- Responding to the physical fact of the disease.
- Taking steps to cope with the reality of the disease.
- Preserving self-concept and relationships with others in the face of the disease.
- Dealing with affective and existential spiritual issues created or reactivated by the disease.

Acute Phase Tasks
- Understanding the disease.
- Maximizing health and lifestyle.
- Maximizing coping strengths and limiting weaknesses.
- Venting feelings (anger, fears, etc.).

- Incorporating the present reality of the diagnosis into one's sense of past and future.

Chronic Phase Tasks
- Managing symptoms and side effects.
- Carrying out heath regimens.
- Preventing and managing health crises.
- Managing stress and examining coping.
- Maximizing social support and minimizing isolation.
- Normalizing life in the face of the disease.
- Dealing with financial concerns.
- Preserving self concept.
- Redefining relationships with others throughout the course of the disease.
- Venting feelings (anger, fears, etc.).
- Finding meaning in suffering, chronic illness, uncertainty, and decline.

Terminal Phase Tasks
- Dealing with symptoms, discomfort, pain and incapacitation.
- Managing health procedures and institutional stress.
- Managing stress and examining coping skills.
- Dealing effectively with caregivers.
- Preparing for death and saying goodbye.
- Preserving self concept.
- Preserving appropriate relationships with family and friends.
- Venting feelings (anger, fears, etc.).
- Finding meaning in life and death.

The pastoral caregiver needs to have two important objectives that serve as a framework for the pastoral care offered to the seriously ill: First, give the person permission to pass away from every important person s/he will leave behind when s/he dies. The achievement of this first objective is more a function of the people in the person's environment than of the person himself/ herself. Most responsible people will realize the burden they place on those they leave behind emotionally and financially. Although death may be inevitable, s/he may still have feelings of guilt for leaving personal duties unfinished, even when it is not in his/her power to do otherwise. For this reason, the pastoral caregiver needs to strive to help enable all the important people in the person's life to grant him/her permission to die. This permission is given verbally, but it also comes in the form of reconciliation, honesty and giving, which allows the dying person to know that even though s/he will be missed, s/he still has permission to die. This permission is essential for a dying person.

Second, enable the person to voluntarily let go of every person and possession in his/her life. This second objective is that of enabling the person to voluntarily let go of all that s/he holds dear in life. Although Jesus Christ urges people to not hold onto the things of this world (see Matthew 6), few (even believers) ever completely achieve that type of life style.

Communicating with the Seriously Ill

Interpersonal communication regarding death and dying has become an increasingly important area in the field of thanatology, wherein research has addressed the critical role of open communication in facilitating the positive processing of a death loss. Being able to communicate honestly about the quality or length of one's life, the disease process, and one's feelings about faith, family members or friends is of utmost importance.

The benefits of open communication are clear. Relationships that allow for communication about death often precede healthy adjustment. Researchers have found that the emotional impact of being labeled as "dying" is directly related to the quality and openness of the communication between the dying individual and others. If open communication is not achieved, then caregivers operate on preconceptions rather than the dying individual's actual thoughts and feelings.

Factors Blocking Good Communication
- Not wanting to face the reality of the death (in other words, always changing the subject).

- Not having the time to become involved (which can be seen by family withdrawing from and avoiding the person).
- Not feeling emotionally able to handle the intensity of the situation (in other words, a fear about discussing death and dying).
- The meaning of the words may not be clear since the terms used may have different meanings for each person.
- Non-verbal signals (in other words, closed body language and no eye contact).
- Strained relationships that make it hard to be open and honest.
- A tendency to judge or to critically evaluate statements that are made.
- A lack of trust.
- An inability or unwillingness to listen empathically.
- Cultural barriers.
- Manipulation.
- Defensive listening.
- Non-accepting tone of voice.
- Pre-occupation with self.
- Inadequate pain management and/or the effects of medication.

Factors Needed for Good Communication
- Appropriate tone of voice.
- Active (empathic) listening skills.
- Good eye contact.
- Sharing of feelings as well as thoughts.
- Clarification of meaning.
- Verbal prompts to encourage talking.

Suggestions for Being Physically Present to the Patient or Resident

- Face them squarely and on same eye level (for good eye contact).
- Adopt an open posture (in other words, no crossed arms).
- Lean toward them.
- Try to be relaxed (smile).

- Show facial expression that indicates you are listening.
- Nod to encourage talking.
- Touch (for example, hold a hand) when appropriate. Dying people sometimes feel "untouchable" so touch can be a meaningful way to communicate care and comfort.

Being with Family of a Dying Person

Facing a serious illness can be a frightening experience, even for the most stable and secure families. There's no "right" way for a family to react or cope. Each family is unique, and each member of the family will have his or her own strengths and vulnerabilities. Identifying and building on the family's strengths is an important part of understanding the vulnerable areas and building in extra support where it is needed. Each member will need time to find his/her own way and own comfort level, without pressure to conform to another's coping style.

Factors that Affect a Family's Reactions

There are several factors that can affect a family's reaction to serious illness.

The Life Stage of the Family. A very young family may not have experienced crises together before now. They may have less confidence in their ability to cope. Families with children will face coping with the children's needs and reactions while also trying to keep their own lives as normal and secure as possible. This may add a lot of stress to their lives. Older families may have experience in handling a crisis, but they may not have the physical stamina they need to cope.

The Presence of Other Stressors in the Family. Financial problems, martial or behavior problems, lack of available support from family and friends, and any other problems that existed before the illness can become even more intense at this time.

The Family Role of the Ill Person. If the dying person is the primary wage earner or the "family executive," there may be financial changes as well as the need for someone else to take on the leadership role. If the ill person is the wife or mother, many household responsibilities may have to be reassigned. The "balance" of the family system changes and they must all adjust.

The Nature of the Illness. Illness that affects a person's appearance, personality, cognitive ability, or ability to function fairly normally will involve many emotional reactions, as well as practical changes. If hospitalization is required, there is more disruption to the family. If the prognosis is uncertain, or the illness involves a process of remission and recurrence, anxiety is usually increased. Families may need support as they experience the confusing ebb and flow of hope and fear, of trying to stay close while also preparing to let go.

Patterns of Family Interaction

There are four patterns of family interaction in response to a life-threatening illness.[9]

Closed Awareness. The dying person does not recognize that death is impending, although other people may know. In general, closed awareness does not allow for open communication about the illness or the probability of death.

Suspected Awareness. The person suspects that the prognosis is death, but this has not been verified by those who know. The dying person may try to confirm or deny his/her suspicions by testing family members, friends and medical personnel in an effort to illicit information known by others, but not openly shared. Despite the secrecy, however, the person is aware that the illness is severely disrupting the family's usual style of relating and may sense others' fearfulness or anxiety about his/her condition, thus tending to confirm the suspicion in the person's mind.

Mutual Pretense. Everyone, including the dying person, recognizes the fact that death will be the outcome, but all act as if the person will recover. Mutual pretense may be practiced right up to the end. The pattern of mutual pretense usually begins early. Subtle signals are communicated among family members that the method used to cope with the crisis is to pretend that things are normal.

Open Awareness. The likelihood of death is openly acknowledged and discussed. Such openness does not necessarily make death easier to accept, but it does offer the possibility of sharing support in ways that would not otherwise be available.

Emotional Reactions of Family Members

Families may react (at the time of diagnosis or during the ongoing crisis) by drawing close together, but they may find it difficult to stay close, to be on their "best behavior," if the illness continues for an extended time. This may produce feelings of disappointment, guilt, anger, and fear. Fears can escalate, including fears for the health of other family members or oneself, as well as fears of death. It is common for people to convert their feelings of fear and sadness into anger. It is easier to respond helpfully when the real, underlying feeling is understood.

It is normal to ask, "Why me?" or "Why my family?" Some family members, especially children, may believe the illness is a punishment from God. It is not uncommon for serious illness to prompt people to question the meaning of life as well as their religious beliefs. This is often upsetting and guilt-producing, but it can lead to an even stronger, more mature, belief system.

Children almost always engage in magical thinking and may believe the illness was caused by something they did or even something they thought. It's important to listen to their thoughts and help them understand that they are not responsible for the illness. They also need to be assured that, as much as possible, their lives will go on normally.

Many people struggle with feelings of guilt and regret, criticizing themselves for past misunderstandings with the ill person. They expect themselves to respond to a life and death situation with constant strength, compassion, patience, and positive thinking. This isn't possible! Sad feelings are normal. Anger is normal. Human relationships are never perfect because human beings are never perfect. Try to help them accept their feelings and to find ways to express them in ways that are acceptable to them.

When a family understands that it is normal for relationships to change when someone becomes seriously ill, they will be less apt to misinterpret the changes, or to feel rejected and frightened.

Opposing Tasks of Family Members

The following are some of the opposing tasks that family members will struggle with, according to Therese Rando, a clinical psychologist, thanatologist and traumatologist[10]:

- Holding on to the patient in opposition to letting go.
- Increasing attachment to the patient during the illness versus starting to detach from the patient in terms of his/her existence in the future.
- Remaining involved with the patient against separating from the patient.
- Planning for life after the death of the patient versus not wanting to betray the patient by considering life in his/her absence.
- Communicating feelings to the patient as opposed to not wanting to make the patient feel guilty for dying or feeling bound to this world when the patient needs to let go.
- Balancing support for the patient's increased dependency versus supporting the patient's continued need for autonomy.
- Focusing on the past and recollecting with the patient versus focusing on the future.
- Redistributing family roles and responsibilities in opposition to not wanting to do anything that would call attention to or cause more losses for the patient.
- Taking care of the patient's needs versus taking care of one's own needs.
- Being immersed in participating in the patient's care versus living one's own life.
- Experiencing the full intensity of feelings involved in anticipatory grief as opposed to trying not to become overwhelmed.
- Focusing on the patient as a living person in opposition to remembering that the patient is dying.
- Continuing reinvestment in the patient who has multiple remissions and relapses and who is going to die anyway versus not reinvesting as much anymore.

- Treating the patient as one always has in the past versus taking into account the patient's situation and treating him/her differently.
- Rushing to create memorable experiences in the patient's last days and pushing for as much meaning as possible in the time remaining as opposed to allowing nature to take its course, reminiscing, and simply being present with the patient.
- Identifying a loss so it can be grieved by the patient versus focusing more positively on the remaining potentials.

Responding to the Seriously Ill

Listen

This is probably the most important ministry activity we can do. We need to encourage them to share their story with us by saying something like, "Please, go on," or "Tell me more." This lets them know that we are interested in hearing their story. Sharing their story, though painful, helps them sort out their feelings and promotes healing by sharing an important experience with someone who cares. If they pause, wait silently for them to continue. Never force them to talk about it. Allow them to proceed at their own pace.

Look

Maintain good eye contact. They may have difficulty sustaining eye contact with us, but we will be sending a nonverbal message that says we are comfortable sharing their grief if we continue to make them the primary focus of our compassionate attention.

Affirm

Respect their thoughts and feelings even if they aren't exactly what we think they should be. This is not a good time to attempt to correct faulty thinking; instead, focus on comfort.

Emote

It's okay to show emotions if we feel the need to cry. We may think that our crying will make them feel worse. However, shared tears are a precious gift and often they are the only appropriate response to a crisis (John 11:35; Romans 12:15b).

Find a balance between the professional goal of "helping someone in need" and the relational goal of "sharing the dying experience."

Hug and Touch

If words aren't easy, a hug or hand on the shoulder or holding a hand can say it all. People in grief often need much more meaningful touching than usual. This includes the males in the family. They are often the forgotten grievers. But only reach out and touch someone when it's appropriate and you have permission to do so.

Replenish Ourselves

We are able to meet their needs to about the same extent our own needs are met. We need to know our own limitations. For example, donating our blood is a great gift for others; however, we never give it all at once!

Tips to Remember when Visiting the Seriously Ill

We need to leave our personal problems and fears at the front door. Be there for the individual and focus on them. We can't "fix" what is going on. "Being there" for them (pastoral presence) is what is really important.

Keep in mind the importance and power of touch. Holding a hand, stroking an arm softly, or simply patting the person's shoulder can be soothing and reaffirming for the person.

Keep body language in mind. Convey caring with an open posture and good eye contact. Sit or stand close and lean forward toward the patient or resident.

Listen. Again, this is an important task. We must focus our attention on what they are saying. Encourage them to talk. Ask for clarification if we need it. We do not need to feel like we must have all the "right answers" to everything. We need to give ourselves permission to be silent. This often gives the person an opening to reflect and continue speaking.

We must be real in expressing our own emotions. It is important to feel that we can laugh or cry with someone who is seriously ill. At the same time, we need to be careful to keep our focus on meeting the person's needs, not our own. We must not "dump" our own fears or grief on the sick person so that they feel they must comfort us. It is okay to say that we are uncomfortable or that we don't know what to say, or even that we wish we could make things better.

Be familiar with Dr. Kubler-Ross' five "stages" (phases) of death and dying.

Remember that hearing is the very last sense to go. So continue to express love and positive statements to a person who appears non-responsive (comatose).

We need to keep our visits brief if the person is tired.

Questions for Review

1. How would you describe the five seasons of the pre-death grief process?
2. What is one practical way to respond to these seasons?
3. What are some tips to remember in coming alongside the seriously ill?

Questions for Reflection

1. If you find yourself feeling uneasy when visiting a seriously ill patient or resident, what are some of the factors you need to consider? How can you prepare effectively for

visiting the seriously ill? Record your insights in a journal and discuss with a confidant and/or the training team.

2. When a dying person wants to unburden his/her heart about past failures, sins, or unhappiness, explain reasons it is important for you to listen without judging them? Record your insights in a journal and discuss with a confidant and/or the training team.
3. What should you do if you are in the room and the person dies and the family is present? Discuss this possibility with the training team.
4. Describe the difference between accepting the truth of impending death and a hopeless resignation to it.
5. Discuss with the training team ways in which you could be helpful to the family at the time of death of their loved one. How would your assistance differ if the person was:

- A small child?
- An elderly patient or resident?
- A young father?
- A teenager?

Chapter Resources

Albers, Gregg R. *Counseling the Sick and Terminally Ill*. Dallas: Word Pub., 1989.

Anderson, Megory. *Attending the Dying: A Handbook of Practical Guidelines*. Harrisburg, PA: Morehouse, 2005.

Bane, J. Donald. *Death and Ministry: Pastoral Care of the Dying and the Bereaved*. New York: Seabury, 1975.

Braham, Mary Ann. *Ministry to the Sick and Dying*. Bloomington, IN: 1st, 2002.

Buckman, Robert, Ruth Gallop, and John Martin. *I Don't Know What to Say: How to Support Someone Who is Dying*. Boston, MA: Little, Brown, 1989.

Callanan, Maggie, and Patricia Kelly. *Final Gifts: Understanding the Special Awareness, Needs, and Communications of the Dying*. New York: Bantam, 1997.

Cauhill, Rita. *The Dying Patient: A Supportive Approach*. Boston, MA: Little, Brown and Company, 1976.

Chapin, Shelley. *Within the Shadow: A Biblical Look at Suffering, Death, and the Process of Grieving*. Wheaton, IL: Victor, 1991.

Cobb, Mark. *The Dying Soul: Spiritual Care at the End of Life*. Buckingham: Open U, 2001.

Davidson, Glen W. *Living With Dying*. Minneapolis, MN: Augsburg, 1975.

Delbene, Ron, Mary Ann Montgomery, and Herb Montgomery. *Into the Light: Ministering to the Sick and Dying*. Nashville, TN: Upper Room, 1988.

Doka, Kenneth J. *Death and Spirituality*. Farmingdale, NJ: Baywood, 1993.

Glaser, Barney G., and Anselm L. Strauss. *Awareness of Dying*. Chicago: Aldine, 1965.

Gram, Robert L. *An Enemy Disguised: Unmasking the Illusion of Meaningful Death*. Nashville: Thomas Nelson, 1985.

Kalina, Kathy. *Midwife for Souls: Spiritual Care for the Dying*. Boston, MA: Pauline & Media, 2007.

Kessler, David. *The Needs of the Dying: A Guide for Bringing Hope, Comfort, and Love to Life's Final Chapter*, New York: Harper, 2007.

Kopp, Ruth. *When Someone You Love Is Dying: A Handbook for Counselors and Those Who Care*. Grand Rapids, MI: Zondervan, 1980.

Kubler-Ross, Elisabeth. *On Death and Dying*. New York: Scribner Classics, 1997.

Kuhl, David. *What Dying People Want: Practical Wisdom for the End of Life*. New York: PublicAffairs, 2002.

Meyer, Charles. *Surviving Death: A Practical Guide to Caring for the Dying & Bereaved*. Mystic, CT: Twenty-third Pub., 1988.

Mills, Liston O. *Perspectives on Death*. Nashville: Abingdon, 1969.

Milner, John. *Struggles in Death: Or Scenes I have Witnessed, And Lessons I have Learned When Visiting the Sick and the Dying*. London: G. Lamb, Primitive Methodist Book Room, 1869.

Moll, Rob. *The Art of Dying: Living Fully into the Life to Come*. Downers Grove, IL: InterVarsity, 2010.

Nouwen, Henri J. M. *Our Greatest Gift: A Meditation on Dying and Caring*. San Francisco, CA: HarperSanFrancisco, 1994.

Platt, Larry A., and Roger Branch. *Resources for Ministry in Death and Dying*. Nashville: Broadman, 1988.

Rando, Therese A. *Grief, Dying, and Death: Clinical Interventions for Caregivers*. Champaign, IL: Research, 1984.

Richards, Larry. *Death and the Caring Community*. Portland, OR: Multnomah, 1980.

Scherzer, Carl J. *Ministering to the Dying*. Englewood Cliffs, NJ: Prentice-Hall, 1963.

Smith, Harold Ivan. *Finding Your Way to Say Goodbye: Comfort for the Dying and Those Who Care for Them*. Notre Dame, IN: Ave Maria, 2002.

Zonnebelt-Smeenge, Susan and Robert C. DeVries. *Living Fully in the Shadow of Death*. Grand Rapids, MI: Baker, 2004.

6

Coming Alongside Grieving People

My grief lies all within,
And these external manners of lament
Are merely shadows to the unseen grief
That swells with silence in the tortured soul.
— William Shakespeare (1564-1616), English poet, playwright

"God blesses those who mourn,
for they will be comforted."
— Jesus (Matthew 5:4, NLT)

Death and Dying

We live in a death-denying society. Everything around us is designed to keep death at bay. We focus on looking young and being healthy in our lifestyles to avoid thinking about getting old or sick or dying. We extol the virtues of those who are considered "old" yet are still active. We make-over corpses to make them look like they're only sleeping, hoping to hear, "He looks so natural" during the viewing. Take time to go through the greeting cards at stationery stores and notice how many of them say something like, "She is just away," or "She is not dead, but only asleep." Medical science is geared to making us live longer. We see death as a failure.

Why is denial of death so common in the American culture? Sociologists and other professionals have suggested a number of reasons, but one factor seems to especially stand out: few people die at home. Most people die in institutions: in acute care hospitals and nursing homes. Even with Hospice care on the rise, it is not very common to hear of a person dying in his or her own home. And, consequently, it is not unusual for family members not to be present when their loved one dies.

Our culture's changing view of what constitutes a family also contributes to the situation. Most children do not live in the same community as their grandparents, let alone in the same house. So children are often denied the experience of witnessing the dying process and rarely are present when a loved one dies. If very young, they are sometimes not even allowed to attend the funeral or memorial service. All of this leads to a culture that increasingly attempts to avoid direct confrontation with death.

Death is no longer a natural part of life, but something to be feared. Yet the fear of death is nothing new. Ever since the days following the Fall, human beings have been in bondage to the fear of death. In Psalm 55:4, David writes, "My heart is severely pained within me, and the *terrors of death* have fallen upon me" (emphasis added).

But what hope the Scriptures do offer! The writer of the letter to the Hebrews tells us that Jesus Christ delivers us from that bondage:

Inasmuch then as the children have partaken of flesh and blood, He Himself likewise shared in the same, that through death He might destroy him who had the power of death, that is, the devil, and release those who through fear of death were all their lifetime subject to bondage (Hebrews 2:14-15).

In John 14:1-6, we read Jesus' promise to go and prepare a place for believers. When we die, it is a new experience for us personally. None of us can know what it will be like until it actually happens. How meaningful and comforting to know that the Lord has already gone on ahead to prepare a place for believers and that they will not be alone there.

Yet a person's fear of death does not mean s/he lacks faith. Fear of death motivates us to take care of ourselves, to look both ways before we cross the street, and to see the doctor when we are sick. In fact, the Scriptures encourage believers to take care of their bodies (1 Corinthians 6:19-20).

It is both normal and understandable that we would not want to face our own death, or the death of a loved one. In the Garden of Gethsemane, the Lord Jesus prayed in agony for the cup of suffering to pass from Him. On the cross He reassured the penitent thief of a place with Him in Paradise. Having faced death Himself, Jesus understands a person's fears and does not condemn someone for experiencing them, although He does want believers to be aware that death has been swallowed up in victory (1 Corinthians 15:54-55).

As pastoral caregivers, we have the great privilege and responsibility of sharing this Gospel hope with the terminally ill and their families. It is important to be sensitive and alert when they indicate that they would like a religious leader to visit. Offer to phone their Pastor, but do not insist upon it. They may be reluctant to have us phone, or they may wish to do it themselves. Be willing to help. Be available if asked. But never be "pushy." As we demonstrate our genuine care and concern for them we are more likely to be welcomed back often.

As in any visit within a healthcare setting, there are a number of factors to consider, but we want to explore them again here in terms of calling on the terminally ill.[1] Because of this death-denying culture, many dying patients and residents are acutely lonely. Their friends and family may begin to stay away for a variety of reasons. For example:

- They cannot deal with their own loss in the face of the person's impending death.
- They are frightened by the things they see in the healthcare setting.

- They are uncomfortable because their loved one's condition confronts them with their own mortality and their own neediness.

As a result, patients and residents are lonely, in need of someone to listen to them, to help them work out their feelings, and to face the very real spiritual crisis of death. We can make a significant contribution to the patient's or resident's well-being at this time, especially if we know how to visit effectively. This means understanding the grief process, as well as being in touch with our own feelings about death and dying.

We may sometimes feel ill at ease when confronted with the totality of a person's terminal illness. Occasionally we may try to cover our uneasiness by being stiff, aloof, or too business-like. Yet giving in to our uneasiness can be harmful to the person, who will certainly be sensitive to it. One way to prevent this from happening is to prepare ourselves before going to see the patient or resident.

Pray for grace to be relaxed. The person will feel our warmth and kindness if we are at ease and comfortable. Be willing to laugh and to chat if the patient or resident is so inclined. Remember that Scripture says laughter is good for our bodies just like medicine helps us when we're ill (Proverbs 17:22). This does not mean that we should be the clown during the visit. Loudness, crudeness, and flippant behavior are out of place and unbecoming to a pastoral caregiver—but we can smile.

Before visiting, we can prepare ourselves by imagining what the room will be like and how the person might look. Will there be IV's, heart monitors, and other equipment in use? Will there be unpleasant odors? How ill will the person look? By thinking about what to expect, we will be better able to confront many of our uncomfortable feelings while still in the comfort of our home or office. Prepare a number of things to say that will relate to what is going on in the outside world, so that we are not at a loss for words when we first enter the person's room.

If we call on a patient or resident whose family is present, we need to introduce ourselves, if we have not done so already. Reassure everyone present that we are standing with them in prayer. This gives comfort not only to the patient or resident, but also to his/her family. We should make our visit brief, but not rushed.

It is sometimes difficult to determine what the best time to visit is. This will often depend upon the routine at the healthcare facility or home and the condition of the patient or resident. Each situation varies, although many pastoral caregivers feel the afternoon is best (and others feel that mornings are best). If possible, develop a pattern of the timing of our visits. This gives the person and family something to look forward to, assuming, of course, that our visits are helpful.

There are times when we should cut our visit short. When we sense that the patient or resident is in pain or uncomfortable, we need to excuse ourselves and return at another time. The person will appreciate our sensitivity and we will be welcomed and privileged to return for further ministry later.

When visiting a patient or resident while other visitors are present, never discuss the person in the third person. For example, don't say, "*He's* feeling better today," or "*She's* not eating anymore." To do so treats the person as though s/he were not even in the room. This conduct assumes that the person cannot speak for him/herself. It tends to make the person feel that s/he is no longer in control of his/her own life and adds to any feelings of victimization and indignity that s/he may be having about the situation.

Do not be the bearer of bad news. Information about train wrecks, airplane crashes, floods, fires, or earthquakes are generally on television and the patient or resident may already be aware of them. If the person has not already learned about them, s/he does not need to hear about them from us. Such information offers nothing positive to the person or family.

By the same token, we should avoid discussing our plans for a social evening or event, such as a big football game we plan to attend or a trip to the mountains. Since the patient or resident is unable to go and may never go again, this can be depressing to the terminal person.

Grief and Loss

Eventually, the terminally ill person will die and there are many ways to help those in grief over that death. The primary emphasis should be on supporting them through this difficult time. The importance of our ministry cannot be overstated, as the griever's emotional, mental, spiritual, and even physical well-being may hang in the balance. We need to "carry" the grief-stricken person like the friends of the paralytic in Mark 2:1-5. Notice that Christ did not emphasize the faith of the sick man, but the faith of his friends.

Our pastoral contribution may make a vital difference in their eventual recovery and re-adjustment into the main stream of life. The following guidelines can help us express our concern and sympathy in a realistic way as we become a CATALYST for healing:

C — Care given out of heart-felt concern.

A — Assessment of total needs of the grieving person that enables us to better anticipate the needs of the bereaved.

T — Tact that is sensitive to difficult situations.

A — Attention to the little extras that make a grieving person feel good about self.

L — Listening love. This is listening for deeper levels of hurt and healing.

Y — Your own relationship with God that in turn influences your attitude and actions toward others.

S — Skill in giving emotional support.

T — Time to be with the grieving person.

Understanding the Grieving Process

If we are going to be helpful to those who are grieving the death of a loved one, it is important that we have a basic understanding of the grieving process.

Basic Insights on Grief

I have found it helpful to use some word pictures to describe a person's grief reaction to a death. For example, I see a loss as similar to a laceration. There is a difference between viewing grieving as being "injured" rather than being "damaged." Being *damaged* implies that something is severely broken (maybe even beyond repair). We usually require a professional to attempt to fix something that is damaged. By contrast, being *injured* (like having a cut) implies only a temporary hurt (a repairable wound). It may or may not require a specialist to attend to it (perhaps stitches). It may leave a noticeable scar behind after it heals. A cut usually involves a process of caring attention in order to promote healing. In other words, grieving a loss is like a cut that, with time and attention, will eventually heal. Grieving is a natural process of healing a deep emotional wound. Even so, sometimes the wound may become infected. This is called complicated grief and we'll discuss that later.

Another symbol for the grieving process might be a compost pile. Most people view a compost pile as something gross, something to be hidden and avoided. However, with time and turning (special attention) the gross pile can be transformed into something enriching and beneficial (it helps the flowers grow and bloom). Like a compost pile, mourning is a natural process of adjusting to change that has the potential of enriching one's life, even though it may appear unpleasant for awhile.

Experiencing grief can be very stressful for the person going through it. But pressure can be pernicious or productive. The Chinese have a character for the word "crisis." It includes the Chinese character wēi (dangerous, perilous) plus the Chinese character jī (incipient moment, crucial point, suitable occasion, opportunity). Within grief is the potential for embitterment (negative consequences—the danger) or increased sensitivity and depth (opportunity for positive growth—the incipient moment).

The events and circumstances of a crisis (grief) experience do not determine the outcome. A person's resources (those within and those without) and personal reactions play a major role in his or her recovery. However, the initial intervention during a crisis can make a significant difference. With this understanding, grief can become a stagnant pond or a flourishing river; a dark, dead-end cave or a promising tunnel; or it can be a place where we get stuck or an adventurous journey.

Keep in mind that present losses link with past losses. Each loss asks its turn to be mourned. There are no short cuts to grieving. All side roads eventually lead back to the main highway of doing personal grief work. In fact, the losses of others may activate personal grief issues. I remember a man whose wife had a stillborn baby. Like many men, he moved on with his life and did not grieve the loss of his son. Eight years later his sister had a stillbirth. The memory of his own loss came flooding back to him and he wept intensely for the loss of both children. It was now time for him to work through his grief that he had put off for the past eight years.

There is actually a difference between "grieving" and "mourning." *Grief* is defined as "intense emotional suffering caused by loss, disaster, misfortune, etc.; acute sorrow; deep sadness." The word is derived from a Latin verb meaning "to burden." The weight of this grief is the composite of thoughts and feelings about a loss we experience within ourselves—it is our *private* (internal) experience of the loss.

Mourning is defined as "to feel or express sorrow." Mourning is when we take the grief on the inside and express it outside ourselves—it is our *public* (external) expression of our loss. The word is derived from a Gothic verb meaning "to be anxious," and it comes ultimately from an Indo-European base word meaning "to remember; to think of." Mourning involves remembering and thinking of the deceased and this makes us feel anxious or uncomfortable with our feelings of loss.

Even though there is a difference in the meaning of the two words, we often use these words as if they were synonyms. Even I do that sometimes. Don't worry about which word you use, but do understand that they do have a different meaning.

Above all, always keep in mind that every person's grief reaction and grieving process is unique. For example, the nature of the loss will make each situation distinctive. Was the death anticipated or unexpected, traumatic, witnessed, viewed as preventable, or one of several recent losses? The kind of the relationship the person had with the deceased will make each situation unique. Was the person very close to the deceased, dependent on the other, ambivalent to or angry with the person (especially if there was any abuse in the relationship), or was their unfinished business? The character and background of the griever is unique. There are distinctions in grief between gender, culture, age, health (both physical and mental), past experience with loss, world view, resiliency, personality, and spirituality. No two people grieve in exactly the same way or at exactly the same pace.

The Cycles of Grief (See Figure 1)

These cycles of grief are not well-defined steps, like going up the rungs of a ladder one step at a time until we reach the top—the end of our grieving. It is a generalized *process* of healing that most everyone experiences.

The first experience in the grief cycle is *shock*. The grieving person might say something like, "I can't believe this is happening!" This is a cycle of unreality, outbursts, disbelief, denial, and/or numbness. It has been compared to a shot of Novocain that numbs our emotional system, or like a bad dream we hope to wake up from soon and find it wasn't real.

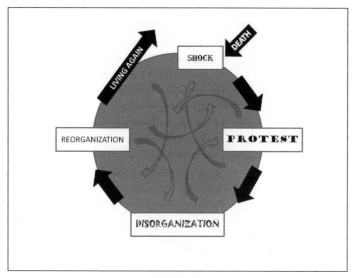

Figure 1
The Cycles of Grief

The second experience in the grief cycle is *protest*. The person in mourning might shout, "This isn't fair!" This phase may include increased shock, preoccupation with thoughts of the deceased, and yearning. This is a cycle of reaction, which might include feelings of:

- Guilt (saying, "If only. . .?"), having self-criticism and either real or imagined regrets.
- Anger (saying, "Why me?"), which can be rational or irrational, turned inward or outward (such as frustration, fear, helplessness, blame, irritation, and resentment).

The third experience is *disorganization*. At this point the grieving person is exclaiming, "I'm falling apart!" This part of the cycle may involve feelings of emptiness, sadness, withdrawal, aimlessness, and depression (with the person saying, "Poor me!"). These normal feelings are merely the symptoms of a very painful wound. It is also a cycle of confusion (like being alone in the middle of a wild, rushing river with nothing to grab hold of; or

127

like feeling we're going crazy). In addition, this part of the cycle may involve yearning (a preoccupation with memories or a shift in perception, for example, hallucinations—having a vision of the person who has died). In addition, it can be a cycle of anxiety (pondering, "Am I going to be okay?") and include decreased socialization (loneliness) and loss of interest.

The final experience of this grief cycle is *reorganization*. At this point the person may say, "I'm finally enjoying living again!" There is no timetable for this recovery. At some point along the journey through grief, the person will eventually regain his/her ability to function as s/he once did (for example, trying new patterns of behavior, discovering new skills, and engaging in new or renewed socialization). They will inevitably resolve and integrate the loss into their life (maybe even finding purpose and meaning in death and life). This acceptance does not mean that they like the loss. It only means that they have learned to live with it as they go on to reinvest their life in new relationships and new dreams.

The Waves of Grief (See Figure 2)

With most grieving people, there is a pattern of emotional highs and lows—of many jagged peaks and valleys—like riding a roller coaster or bobbing up and down in waves. The emotional pain is usually most intense the first three to six months and then it gradually subsides, but often not in a steady manner. The emotional response can *fluctuate* up and down on a daily, even hourly, basis. Around the one-year anniversary, the intensity of the grief can come rushing in with tsunami-like pain that almost rivals the initial feelings of grief at the beginning of the loss.

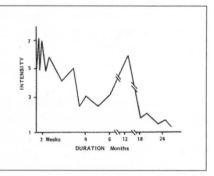

Figure 2
The Waves of Grief:
Shock and Numbness

Please do not make the mistake of telling a grieving person who has had a significant loss only a year or two ago, "You should be over it by now!"

Notice in Figure 2 that emotions regarding the shock of the death don't get back to near-normal until about two years after the death (on average).[2] No average timetable can be set for each person to reach acceptance of a death. Everyone moves through the grieving process at his/her own pace. However, being stuck in a phase or with particular emotions may indicate a blockage in the healing process and might be a signal that help is needed.

Four Tasks of Mourning[3]

Accept the reality of the loss. When someone dies, even if the death is expected, it is hard to believe the person is really gone. The first task of grieving is to face the reality that the person is dead and will not return. A sign that we have aborted this task would include denial, in other words, not believing the person is truly dead and gone. Denying the facts of the loss, the meaning of the loss, or the irreversibility of the loss only serves to prolong the grief process. Though denial is normal immediately after the loss, this illusion is usually short-lived.

Experience the pain of the grief. This task involves allowing ourselves to experience and express our feelings. Anger, guilt, loneliness, anxiety, and depression are among some of the feelings and experiences that are normal during this time. Be assured that the memory of our loved one will continue and the pain will lessen over time. Signs of this task being aborted include acting stoic, in other words, not allowing ourselves to feel or express our feelings openly. Grieving people tend to try to avoid their painful feelings by various ways such as "being strong," moving away, "keeping busy," etc.

Adjust to an environment in which the deceased is missing. This means different things to different people, depending on what the relationship was. Many survivors, especially widowed persons, resent or fear having to develop new skills and to take on roles that were formerly performed by the deceased spouse. In other words, this task involves being willing to do things differently since the deceased will no longer be involved in certain activities. Signs of an aborted task include not adapting, not adjusting to these new roles and a new identity.

Reinvest in living. The final task is to affect an emotional withdrawal from the deceased person so that this emotional energy can be used in continuing a productive life. This does not necessarily mean finding a new spouse, surrogate mother, etc. It does mean re-entering the stream of life without the deceased loved one as we reinvest that emotional energy in other relationships and activities. This is not dishonoring the memory of the deceased and doesn't mean that we love him or her any less or we are forgetting about the person. It simply recognizes that there are other people and things to be loved and we are still capable of loving. Signs of an aborted task would include not loving, but continuing to "walk alone."

Four Key Facts About Grief[4]

The way out of grief is through it. People heal best when they embrace their pain. Time itself will never heal grief—it is what a person does with the time that matters. Everyone must deal with his or her own grief and work through it.

The worst kind of grief is our own. Is it more difficult to say good-bye to a newborn or a teenager or a grandparent? Is it worse to watch someone die "an inch at a time" from a crippling disease or to lose a loved one suddenly and unexpectedly in a tragic accident? Pain is pain! It hurts to say goodbye to a loved one.

Grief is hard work. It's *hard* to admit that a loved one has died. It's *hard* work to vent our strong feelings. And it's *hard* work to release the one who has died.

Effective grief work is not done alone. It should not be kept to ourselves. We need to share our grief with a personal confidant or in a grief support group.

Complicated (or Unhealthy) Grief

When the grief process is *significantly exaggerated, excessively prolonged* and/or *seriously interferes* with a person's capacity to function in life roles, some degree of pathology (infection of the wound) may be assumed and consultation with a professional therapist is earnestly advised.

The following symptoms should receive professional help if they occur:

- Any self-destructive thoughts or behavior.
- Inability to sleep at all.
- Significant weight loss or gain.
- Hallucinations and/or delusions.
- Panic or anxiety attacks.
- Unusual physical pain or symptoms.
- Hyperactivity such as overworking, taking on major new responsibilities, compulsive shopping, gambling, sexual activity and/or traveling.
- Feeling so completely overwhelmed they're unable to get out of bed or be active.
- Over usage of medications.
- Excessive use of alcohol.
- Use of illegal drugs.

The following symptoms should receive professional help if they are severe and persist for longer than one month following the death:

- Gross denial of reality of the loss.
- Out of control anger or rage.
- Intense shame.
- Severe depression.
- Severe anxiety and fears.

Alan Wolfelt, Director for Loss and Life Transition in Fort Collins, CO, explains unhealthy grief responses that can be characterized through five avoidance patterns.[5]

The *Postponer* is the person who believes that if you delay the expression of your grief it will hopefully go away over a period of time. But it doesn't! It is through expression that healing comes. Postponement only causes the grief to build up to volcanic proportions.

The *Displacer* is the person who takes the expression of grief away from the loss itself and displaces the feelings in other directions. For example, the person may complain of difficulty at work or in relationships with other people. Or the person may be chronically agitated and upset at even the most minor of events. This places stress on personal relationships.

The *Replacer*. This is someone who takes the emotions that were invested in the relationship that ended in death and reinvests these emotions prematurely in another relationship or in overworking.

The *Minimizer* is someone who is aware of feelings of grief, but when the feelings are actually felt, the person works to minimize the feelings, diluting them through a variety of rationalizations. This is typically an intellectual process in which words substitute for the expression of authentic feelings in order to avoid pain at all costs.

The *Somatizer*. This is the person who converts his/her feelings of grief into physical symptoms. By taking on the "sick role," people around the person legitimize his/her very real need to be nurtured and comforted. The somatizer often fears that if s/he was to express his/her true feelings of grief, people would pull away and leave the person feeling abandoned.

Responding to Grieving Families

Before reading this next section, answer the following questions: What's hardest about being with those who are grieving? Once you have answered that question, now answer this one: What do you think they need/want from us?

Before we can help someone else deal with their grief, we need to first experience fully and deal adequately with our own grief issues. We need to do our own "grief work" so we can see and come alongside someone else's pain. Otherwise, their loss will function as a mirror of our own pain. In other words, we will see our own grief instead of theirs, which will make it very difficult for us to effectively come alongside them and comfort them because our pain is now getting in the way.

Convey Caring

Remember: We can't "fix it" (we can't give them their loved one back and make it all better) but we can imprint a memory of caring alongside their painful loss. How? Here are seven be-attitudes that will help us convey caring to the grieving person.

Be Genuine. This is having our actions be consistent with our words. The truly genuine person is unwavering in his/her values or attitudes, aware of his/her own emotions, and willing to share of himself or herself and his/her own feelings.

Be Empathetic. Empathy is viewing and understanding the situation from *their* perspective, getting a feeling for what *they* are going through.

Be Warm. This means showing friendliness and consideration through facial expression, tone of voice, gestures, a relaxed posture, and good eye contact.

Be Available. Being accessible means being open to come alongside and listen to them tell their story, to sit with them, and to weep with them.

Be a Sensitive Listener. This involves trying to understand their feelings and hearing what they are really saying, without making judgmental or critical comments. Listening encourages the person to talk.

Be an Affirmer. Affirmation is encouraging them to feel what they feel. It is validating their loss and their feelings by giving them permission to openly express their grief.

Be Patient. It will take time. They won't "snap out of it" quickly, so they need someone to persevere with them over the long haul.

Hurtful Clichés versus Healing Comments

When coming alongside grieving people we need to avoid saying hurtful clichés and quoting "fix it" Bible verses and, instead, offer healing comments. When the emotional wound of death is fresh and tender, clichés and Bible verses are simply too superficial. Instead, those who are grieving need to hear reassurances that their suffering is genuine and normal and that the life of their loved one stood for something. Statements that validate a void has been made in their life, or that the deceased person will be missed, are statements that are normally appreciated. Saying, "God needed another angel," is not usually soothing to most people (and it's not biblically true). Making a comment like, "Be grateful for the time you did have with him/her," is seldom perceived as a positive statement at the moment of death.

Here are some of the *hurtful clichés* that I have heard while involved in chaplaincy care (and some Scripture that they may tend to use along with the insensitive statement).

- Time will heal (Ecclesiastes 3:1, 4).
- God never gives us more than we can handle (1 Corinthians 10:13).
- You must be strong (Galatians 6:5).
- You're holding up so well (Proverbs 14:13).
- This is God's will for you (Romans 8:28).
- This is a blessing in disguise (Genesis 50:20).
- You need more faith (Matthew 21:22).
- You need to get right with the Lord (Isaiah 53:5).
- God showed me a verse for you (Hesitation 4:1).
- You shouldn't feel this way (1 Thessalonians 4:13).
- You need to accept what happened and get on with your life (Philippians 3:13).
- You should be glad it wasn't worse. . .at least you have insurance. . .other children (said to a mother who just had her child die). . .your arms (said to someone who had just lost both legs), etc.
- I know how you feel.
- Let me know if I can do anything.

Here are some *healing comments* that might be said instead of the other statements.

- You must feel as if the pain will never end.
- This must seem overwhelming to you at this time.
- Don't feel you need to be strong for me.
- It's normal to cry (be angry, etc.).
- Some things just don't make any sense.
- I'm sorry this had to happen.
- It must be hard to trust God right now.
- There are no words to express my sorrow for you.
- Tell me what you're thinking/feeling.
- It's normal to feel like this.
- God gives strength to get through each day. He will be there for you. . .and so will I.
- What's hardest for you about dealing with this?
- I can only imagine how you must feel. Tell me about it.
- I'll come by tomorrow with groceries (or dinner), what time is good for you?

Offer Helpful Actions Instead of Empty Words

We need to begin where they are, not where we think they ought to be.

Listen to them. Encourage them to talk about their grief. Someone has said, "A joy shared seems to double it; a sorrow shared seems to half it."

Give meaningful touch. When appropriate, this means holding a hand while they share painful memories, placing a hand on their shoulder while they cry, or giving them an arm around the shoulder hug. Few things heal wounded spirits better than the balm of supportive touch.

Pray for them and with them. This involves praying simply and specifically for the personal needs we are aware that they have and will face.

Assess their needs. We might ask, "Who's going to be there for you over the next two months?" Or we might inquire, "How do you normally cope with this kind of situation?"

Offer practical assistance. Like what? Offer to help them make some phone calls. Give them resources they can read that will help them understand the grieving process¾a small booklet is better than a big book.

Refer them to a grief recovery support group and offer to go with them. Refer them to a grief counselor (a clergy person or a professional therapist).

In Conclusion

Let me close this discussion with some wise words shared with me years ago by Marilyn Gryte, a nurse at a women's hospital in Oregon, speaking about coming alongside parents after the death of their baby:

There is no way to soften devastating news; no way to ease the wrenching pain. But it is incredibly important that it be done by someone who cares enough to try.

What that means to me is that you don't need to be an expert in order to come alongside and comfort a grieving person; all you need to do is be available to show love and compassion. I'm confident that with the help of God's Spirit within you—the Comforter—you can do that.

Questions for Review

1. Can you explain the difference between "grief" and "mourning"?
2. How would you describe the waves of grief to someone?
3. What are the four tasks of mourning?
4. Name some clichés and explain why they are perceived as hurtful (or not helpful) by those who are grieving?

Questions for Reflection

1. If possible, interview someone who has had a family member die. Ask about his or her grief reactions and what

support was most comforting to him/her. After spending several minutes in Bible study, reflection and prayer on what you learned, write a summary of your insights from this conversation and discuss those insights with a confidant and/or the training team.

2. Have you ever been seriously ill or injured? If you have not yet had this experience, is there someone close to you — a family member or friend — who has? Answer these questions in terms of how you reacted to the situation.

- Describe your feelings at the time. Were you afraid? Peaceful? Worried?
- What was most helpful to you at the time?
- What was least helpful?

What do you learn about pastoral care from this experience? Discuss your insights with the training team.

3. Describe the first time you had to deal with death. How did this experience affect you? Did you have feelings that you would think of as negative? What took these feelings away? How has being a Christian played a role in developing your attitude about death? Write a summary of your insights and discuss them with a confidant and/or the training team.

4. A small child in the healthcare facility has died unexpectedly from a sudden illness, and the parents are distraught. After you identify yourself to the parents, the mother asks you to read scripture to comfort her. What do you read? Then she asks you, "Do all babies and children go to heaven when they die?" How do you respond?

5. In 1 Thessalonians 4:13-18, Christians are admonished not to grieve as if we had no hope. Explain to a confidant and/or the training team what this means to you and how this understanding might impact how you come alongside those who are grieving.

Chapter Resources

Atchison, Liam, and Precious Atchison. *Grief*. Colorado Springs, CO: NavPress, 1994.

Bailey, Robert W. *The Minister and Grief*. New York: Hawthorn, 1976.

Bayly, Joseph. *The Last Thing We Talk About* (formerly called *The View From a Hearse*). Elgin, IL: David C. Cook, 1973.

Bowman, George W. *Dying, Grieving, Faith, and Family: A Pastoral Care Approach*, Binghamton, NY: Haworth Pastoral, 1998.

Bregman, Lucy. *Death in the Midst of Life: Perspectives on Death from Christianity and Depth Psychology*. Grand Rapids, MI: Baker, 1992.

Briggs, Lauren. *What You Can Say When You Don't Know What to Say: Reaching Out to Those Who Hurt*. Eugene, OR: Harvest House, 1985.

Centering Corporation. Omaha, NE. www.centering.org.
They list over 600 resources for the bereaved.

Chesser, Barbara Russell. *Because You Care: Practical Ideas for Helping Those Who Grieve*. Waco, Texas: Word Pub., 1987.

Compassion Books. Burnsville, NC. www.compassionbooks.com.
They have over 400 mail-order books, audios and videos on death and dying, bereavement and change, comfort, healing, inspiration and hope.

Davidson, Glen W. *Understanding Mourning: A Guide to Those Who Grieve*. Minneapolis, MN: Fortress, 1984.

Deits, Bob. *Life After Loss: A Personal Guide Dealing with Death, Divorce, Job Change and Relocation*. Tucson, AZ: Fisher, 1992.

Doka, Kenneth J., ed. *Living With Grief: Who We Are, How We Grieve*. Washington, DC: Hospice Foundation of America, 1999.

Grief Share. www.griefshare.org.
They offer support groups and resources. Check it out.

Kinnamen, Gary. *My Companion Through Grief*. Ann Arbor, MI: Servant Pub., 1996.

Kolf, June Cerza. *How Can I Help? Reaching Out to Someone Who Is Grieving*. Grand Rapids, MI: Baker, 1989.

Komp, Diane M. *Hope Springs from Mended Places: Images of Grace in the Shadows of Life*. Grand Rapids, MI: Zondervan, 1994.

Kubler-Ross, Elisabeth, and David Kessler. *On Grief and Grieving: Finding the Meaning of Grief Through the Five Stages of Loss*. New York: Scribners, 2005.

Kuenning, Delores. *Helping People Through Grief*. Minneapolis, MN: Bethany House, 1987.

Larson, Dale G. *The Helper's Journey: Working With People Facing Grief, Loss, and Life-Threatening Illness*. Champaign, IL: Research, 1993.

Linn, Eric. *I Know Just How You Feel: Avoiding the Clichés of Grief*. Cary, IL: Publisher's Mark, 1986.

Meyer, Charles. *Surviving Death: A Practical Guide to Caring for the Dying & Bereaved*. New London, CT: Twenty-third Pub., 1991.

Miller, James E. *How Can I Help? 12 Things To Do When Someone You Know Suffers A Loss*. Fort Wayne, IN: Willowgreen, 1994.

New England Center for Loss & Transition. www.neclt.org. They list several resources.

O'Toole, Donna. *Healing and Growing through Grief*. Burnsville, NC: Mountain Rainbow Pub., 1993.

Rando, Therese A. *Grief, Dying, and Death: Clinical Interventions for Caregivers*. Champaign, IL: Research, 1983.

Robinson, Haddon W. *Grief: Comfort for Those Who Grieve and Those Who Want Help*. Grand Rapids, MI: Discovery House, 1996.

Schoeneck, Therese S. *Hope for Bereaved: Understanding, Coping and Growing Through Grief*. Syracuse, NY: Therese S. Schoeneck, 1990.

Westberg, Granger E. *Good Grief: A Constructive Approach to the Problem of Loss*. Philadelphia: Fortress, 1971.

Wiersbe, Warren W., and David W. Wiersbe. *Comforting the Bereaved*. Chicago: Moody, 1985.

Williams, Donna, and Joann Sturzl. *Grief Ministry: Helping Others Mourn*. San Jose, CA: Resource, 1990.

Williams, Robert A. *Journey Through Grief*. Nashville: Thomas Nelson, 1991.

Wolfelt, Alan D. *Death and Grief: A Guide for Clergy*. New York: Brunner-Rutledge, 1988.

Wright, H. Norman. *Recovering from the Losses of Life*. Tarrytown, New York: F. H. Revell, 1991.

7

Handling Emergencies

It's queer how ready people always are with advice in any real or imaginary emergency, and no matter how many times experience has shown them to be wrong, they continue to set forth their opinions, as if they had received them from the Almighty!
— Anne Sullivan (1866-1936), American teacher[1]

Those who live in the shelter of the Most High
will find rest in the shadow of the Almighty. . .
*The L*ord *says, "I will rescue those who love Me.*
I will protect those who trust in My name.
When they call on Me, I will answer;
I will be with them in trouble.
I will rescue them and honor them.
I will satisfy them with a long life
and give them My salvation.
— Psalm 91:1, 14-16 (NLT)

I f you make a commitment to be available for coming alongside the hurting as a pastoral caregiver, then you will be faced with emergency situations. Handling emergencies requires compassion, quick and insightful assessment skills, and psychological and spiritual alignment with patients or residents, their family members, and the healthcare staff. This chapter deals with screening emergency calls, handling patient and resident emergencies, and family emergencies.

Screening "After Hours" Calls

The purpose of screening *after hour* calls is so that one can provide a systematic, proportional response to these emergencies. The ringing of your cell phone does not automatically necessitate an immediate trip to the healthcare facility. Before acting, carefully assess the nature and severity of the situation. Prudent screening of these *after hours* calls will enable the pastoral caregiver to guard one's time off and to avoid compassion fatigue.

Being on call 24/7/365 does not mean that we should rush to the healthcare facility every time we are called. Before responding to a call, we will want to ask what is the religious background of the patient or resident and if the person in need has a desire for a specific type of clergy person (for example, a Priest, Rabbi, or Imam). There are still times when we may be called even when a Priest is desired.

If possible, ask to be connected with the nursing station from which the request originated. Ask the nurse on duty whether or not visiting the next day might meet the need. Ask if we can talk to the person in need over the phone. Sometimes praying over the phone and promising that we will try to visit the next day will be sufficient. If it is necessary for us to go in, give the approximate time it will take us to reach the facility or home. Sometimes the family who requested us will not want to wait the length of time it may take us to get to the facility or home.

Following a screening process will save us from many unnecessary trips to the healthcare facility and enable us to focus on the cases where our presence is important.

Patient and Resident Emergencies[2]

An emergency or critical incident is usually an event that places in jeopardy a patient's or resident's life and well-being. Even so, the same event that may be a crisis for one person may not be so significant for another person. This depends on several factors, particularly their perception of the event itself. This may be shaped by their past experience, personality, coping skills, perception of personal resources to handle the situation, perception of support from others, spiritual well-being, mental and emotional well-being, physical health, and other factors.

The crisis facing the patient or resident involves not only the physical ailment or disease, but also the attending psychological and spiritual imbalance they may be experiencing. In times of such emergencies, the pastoral caregiver's role is to provide spiritual and emotional first aid. Two *yardsticks*[3] can be employed to aid the pastoral caregiver in providing strategic and timely spiritual and emotional first aid.

First, the pastoral caregiver needs to measure or assess the nature and severity of the critical incident or emergency that the patient or resident faces. Second, the pastoral caregiver needs to assess the impact of the critical incident on the patient or resident and/or any family members or friends present.

Yardstick #1: Assessment of the nature and severity of the critical incident involves answering several questions

There are five questions that we will want to answer in order to assess the nature and severity of the critical incident (emergency).

1. What type of critical incident was it?
Was it an injury from an accident? The traumatic stress level is usually higher due to the suddenness and unexpectedness of an injury resulting from an accident.

Was it a planned surgery? The traumatic stress level does not have the same sense of unexpectedness in terms of the event occurring; however, the surgery may be life-threatening or it may be very frightening to the person.

Was it an injury from a perpetrated attack? The traumatic stress level is often high because of the unexpectedness and surprise element and because of the event being a willful, premeditated, and violent act.

Was it an injury from a natural disaster? The traumatic stress level may be high, depending on the severity of the injury and the nature of the disaster.

2. What persons were involved with the critical incident?

Was the patient brought to the ER by ambulance or by family members?

Was the patient brought to the hospital alone?

Are family members and/or friends present or on the way?

3. What was the severity of the injury from the critical incident?

Did the person receive only minor abrasions or a simple bone fracture?

Was there a sudden cardiac arrest or stroke?

Was there an unexpected diagnosis of cancer or some other serious, chronic illness?

Is there mental impairment, which can be due to psychosis, hallucinations, drugs, dementia, etc.?

4. Who was impacted and/or injured at the scene of the critical incident?

For example, a male patient slumps down in an unconscious state in his bathroom. His wife finds him and calls for paramedics. The patient and his wife are the primary shock victims at the scene of the critical incident.

5. Who was impacted by the shock wave of the news of the critical incident and injury sustained or death that occurred off the scene of the critical incident?

For example, the wife, who discovered her husband unconscious in the bathroom, called other family and friends. Those family and friends, whom the wife notified, are secondary shock victims *off* (away from) *the scene* of the critical incident.

The other family members and friends of the unconscious man, when contacted by the wife, may experience a high level of distress depending on the closeness of the relationship and life-threatening condition of the person.

Yardstick #2: Assessment of the impact of the critical incident upon the person and/or any family member or friend present involves several observations

There are some observations we will need to make in order to assess the impact of a critical incident on someone.

Observe the following five items in order to notice the symptoms of traumatic stress expressed by the impacted person:

Speech: Is the person talking rapidly, haltingly, or not at all?

Emotion: What kind of emotion and at what level is the emotion being expressed? An impacted person may be at one extreme or another, either non-responsive verbally and emotionally flat, or yelling wildly and explosively emotional.

Appearance: Does the person look disheveled? Does the person have blood on their hands or clothes?

Activity Level: Is the person hyper-vigilant, or jumpy, or frozen with no energy at all?

Alertness: Thoughts will tend to be concrete. They may have little abstraction ability. Their thinking may be tangential or in random order. Memory and decision-making are often impaired.

By observing the impact of the critical incident on the person's speech, emotion, appearance, activity, and alertness, we will be able to recognize traumatic stress symptoms that fall into five domains: 1) physical, 2) cognitive, 3) emotional, 4) behavioral, and 5) spiritual.

Almost immediately after the impact of the critical incident, traumatic stress symptoms will develop in the physical, cognitive, and emotional domains. After a few days, the intensity of the traumatic stress symptoms in the physical, cognitive, and emotional domains will subside. After this, behavioral and spiritual relationships symptoms of traumatic stress will begin to appear. Spiritual crisis assessment and intervention needs to occur not only shortly after a critical incident, but also a few days later to check for impairment in horizontal relationships with family, friends, and co-workers, and for impairment in the patient's vertical relationship with God.

The domains of traumatic stress symptoms include *physical symptoms*, such as a vacant stare, a rapid heart rate and fast breathing, excessive sweating, chills, or vomiting.

We will observe *cognitive symptoms*, like confusion in thinking, trouble in making decisions, trouble with memory and recall, and alertness (high or low).

There will also be *emotional symptoms*, for instance, shock, anger, fear, despair, and panic.

We will observe *behavioral symptoms* of impairment in horizontal relationships, such as eating too little or too much, sleeping too little or too much, poor hygiene, and withdrawal from or severing of relationships.

Finally, there will be *spiritual symptoms* of impairment in their vertical relationship with God, for instance, feeling like God has abandoned them, finding it hard to pray, no spirit of thankfulness, and no sense of hope.

SAFER-R Model[4]

After using the two *yardsticks* to measure the nature and severity of the critical incident (emergency) and to assess the degree of impact on those involved, we will have the opportunity, as a pastoral caregiver, to provide spiritual crisis intervention appropriate to the assessment.

The majority of spiritual crisis interventions that a pastoral caregiver will make will be one-on-one. The most effective individual crisis intervention model is the SAFER-R model of the International Critical Incident Stress Foundation (ICISF). The SAFER-R model is a strategic and systematic interview process by which an ICISF trained interventionist can mitigate the impact of traumatic stress on the person and/or family and improve functioning in relationships.

"**S**" in the SAFER-R model stands for ***Stabilize*** *the individual and acute adverse stress reactions*. We need to take the initiative in introducing ourselves as a pastoral caregiver from our church.

By making good eye-contact and extending a calm and confident greeting, we can begin to build trust and instill hope.

"**A**" in the SAFER-R model stands for *Acknowledge the crisis event and that reactions are due to the event and not personal weakness*. Use closed-ended questions (Who, What, When, or Tell me. . .) to get the person or family member 1) to tell us about the critical incident that they experienced or are experiencing, and 2) to tell us about how the critical incident has impacted them. We need to actively and empathically listen to their story.

"**F**" in the SAFER-R model stands for helping *Facilitate their understanding of the event and normalize their reactions to it*. Help the person recognize that they will be able to rebound from these debilitating symptoms of traumatic stress and return to normal functioning. Note that experiencing post-traumatic stress symptoms after a critical incident is to be expected (it's a normal response) and is not a sign of weakness or failure.

"**E**" in the SAFER-R model stands for *Encourage adaptive coping techniques*. We need to help them identify personal stress management tools that will empower them to cope. We instill hope by being God's ambassador through listening to the person's cry of distress and by offering practical steps of help when appropriate. An example of practical help would be to offer to notify the person's Pastor of the hospitalization.

"**R-R**" in the SAFER-R model stands for *Restore functioning* and *Refer to ongoing care*. As we conclude the conversation with the person and/or family member, we will have assessed and determined 1) if we feel comfortable about concluding the conversation, or 2) if we need to make a referral to support resources (such as a social worker or counselor or Pastor). For example, a patient recovering from a stroke squeezes our hand as we pray for them. Notifying the nurse about the patient's squeezing of our hand would be appropriate since the nurse is tracking the patient's recovery process.

To build trust with the person and/or the family and friends present, and hear accurately their spiritual cries of distress, we need to align spiritually and psychologically with them. By attending to their body language, tone and inflection of voice, and to the emotions that their words evoke within the pastoral caregiver as the

147

listener, the pastoral caregiver will be able to make a paraphrase of their statement. The paraphrase of their statement is one way to connect with them and for them to know that we have heard them. Telling our personal stories in response to their statement inappropriately shifts the focus from them to us.

Family Emergencies

Our Purpose

In coming alongside those in crisis, our purpose as a pastoral caregiver is to provide spiritual care for families during and after the crisis (such as a code blue or a death).

General Protocol

In the *Manual on Hospital Chaplaincy* by the American Hospital Association, it states that:

> *When death occurs in the hospital, the Chaplain should be called. This event has religious significance to almost everyone and calls for ministry to the family; the presence of the hospital pastor communicates the institution's continuing concern and respect for their needs.*[5]

Specific Protocol

When called to come to the bedside of a dying person, or to come to minister to the surviving family, the pastoral caregiver needs to also take time to check on how the healthcare staff is doing with respect to the death of the person. For example, if the patient who died was an 18-month-old baby upon whom the emergency room staff worked for several hours, the staff may need some spiritual crisis intervention after the pastoral caregiver has finished consoling and praying with family members.

Once notified of the emergency, the pastoral caregiver will notify the nurse of his/her estimated time of arrival to the crisis. Be honest in the time it will take to respond. If it takes 30 minutes, say, "I'll be there in 30 minutes." Otherwise, the family will not know when to expect us and may leave.

After regular hours, the pastoral caregiver should be called only for emergencies. Have a pen and paper by the phone. Repeat the information given by the switchboard operator or person contacting you. Find out who contacted the switchboard operator. Whenever possible, speak to the person who made the request.

Upon arriving at the crisis, the pastoral caregiver will check with the nurse or doctor regarding the status of the person and any other important information before locating the family. Do not feel intimidated; simply ask (after identifying who you are), "Would you share with me what is going on?"

Go to the family to see how we might minister to their spiritual and emotional needs. Share our concern and willingness to help them. A good beginning question here would be, "Would you share with me what has taken place here?" If appropriate, the importance of touch may be crucial here (holding a hand or placing a hand on a shoulder).

Listen to them. Listen with your eyes. Good eye contact is vitally important at this time. Forget about looking at your watch. Ignore your phone. Give them permission to react to the situation and to grieve. Try to enter into their world and into their hurt.

Mention out loud who is going to be their support team. We might say something like, "You have some people here that are going to support you through this ordeal. Tom is going to be of help, aren't you Tom?"

If we are in the room with the family when the person dies, we need to excuse ourselves calmly and then go notify the nurse who will in turn find a doctor to officially pronounce the death. If possible, we should be present when the doctor notifies the family that the person has died.

When a patient or resident has died without the family being present, we will want to find out from the nurse whether the body is able to be viewed by the family and then check with the family to see whether they wish to view the body. Keep in mind that if the deceased is a Coroner's case, all tubes (including IVs and the breathing tube) will still be in place and we will need to inform the family about what to expect. We will want to stay with the family while they view the body. Pull the curtains if there are other patients or residents in the room. Protect the family's privacy as much as possible.

If the body has already been removed from the room to the morgue, contact the Nursing Supervisor or Security to arrange for the family to view the body. Accompany the family to the morgue (or other viewing room).

After viewing, take them to another room for privacy. Help in practical ways. Provide a cup of water or juice (avoiding, if possible, drinks with caffeine in it). We may need to assist in dialing the phone for them. Ask, "Can I help you with making any phone calls?"

Find out if any of those present is on any medication or has a history of fainting, dizziness, etc. While giving permission to grieve also watch for extreme grief reactions. Share the importance of the grief process if we feel it would be beneficial. Encourage the adults to allow their children to grieve with them. Allow for periods of silence.

After being with them for an appropriate period of time, leave the room. This gives them permission to grieve in private. Tell them you will be back in a short time.

Return to the room with some water or juice (coffee and tea are stimulants and should probably be avoided at this time). Ask them if there is anything else that we can do to be of help. At some point, after things have calmed down a bit, the pastoral caregiver may say, "God knows that we are frail and weak and He helps us through times of trouble." A verse like Nahum 1:7 or Psalm 46:1 may be helpful to share at this point (or not). A short prayer might be comforting, if indicated (and permission to pray has been granted). Do not pray prematurely.

The pastoral caregiver may assist the family in obtaining any valuables and personal items belonging to the deceased (such as jewelry, clothes, purse/wallet, keys, etc.).

In providing spiritual support to the grieving family, the pastoral caregiver may offer to call the Pastor if they wish. The pastoral caregiver may provide emotional and spiritual support until the Pastor arrives.

The pastoral caregiver may assist the family in making decisions regarding selection of a funeral home and/or making funeral arrangements. Always give them more than one selection. That way it will not seem as though we are in partnership with any particular mortuary. We should be familiar with multiple funeral homes located in the vicinity of our healthcare facility. Encourage them to work out the details together. Give wise counsel, if requested, regarding cost, types of services available, etc. Leave our card with them and let them know of our availability. They may have additional questions, once the initial shock of grief begins to ebb.

Do not let immediate family members drive, if at all possible, following the death. Use family, friends or neighbors to provide transportation. Look for an emotionally stable person who is with the family who may be able to assist us if we need help or are involved with a large family.

After the family has left the healthcare facility, return to the ward and talk with any patients or residents who were aware of the death and/or were in the room of the deceased, as we deem appropriate. Allow them to verbalize their thoughts and feelings and any concerns regarding the death or their own mortality.

Talk with the doctor(s), nurses, ward secretary, etc. to see how they are handling this particular death, if the timing is right to do so. Our expressed concern and support for them is equally as important as with the family and may result in further ministry with them.

Try to follow-up with the family according to their individual needs and support systems they may or may not have. Place a call to the family of the deceased after a week or so has passed. We might want to consider sending a sympathy card that has also been signed by the Pastor. This act of reaching out can be very meaningful to the family.

Four Ways NOT to Respond to an Emergency

There are some who may react to an emergency situation in one of the following profiles, each of which would be considered as an inappropriate response by a pastoral caregiver.

The Joker

Such "comedians" try to use laughter to lighten the tremendous stress of the situation. Unfortunately, they usually employ their humor inappropriately and too frequently, and are often viewed as being insensitive.

The Holy Person

This "saintly" individual attempts to appear super-spiritual instead of simply being human—a fellow struggler. Such a person usually has a Scripture verse for every situation (especially Romans 8:28) and believes that anyone truly trusting in Jesus will never be afraid, worried, sad, angry, etc.

The Guidance Counselor

These "resolvers" have a tendency to want to try and solve (fix) everyone's problem. Through their spiritual counsel, they want to put back into working order anything that seems to be "broken."

The Professional

This "authority" person sees himself or herself as the consummate expert. S/he has a know-it-all attitude and likes to be in control of the situation.

Questions for Review

1. Why do you need to screen after-hours calls?
2. How would you explain the two yardsticks for assessing the needs of someone experiencing a crisis?
3. What is the SAFER-R model?
4. Can you describe one way you should not respond to someone going through a crisis situation?

Questions for Reflection

1. If you have not already done so, visit the Emergency Department (ED) of your local hospital and observe what goes on there. Now spend several minutes in Bible study, reflection and prayer regarding the four profiles mentioned above: Joker, Holy Person, Guidance Counselor, and Professional. Write out your understanding of each of these traits, including whether you see any of these tendencies in yourself. Explain how you may counteract any of these tendencies. Discuss your insights with a confidant and/or the training team.

2. What are some appropriate Scriptures for patients and residents in the following crisis situations:

- One facing life threatening surgery.
- One learning that s/he has cancer.
- One who could die soon.
- One wondering "Why me?"

3. With violence increasing at an alarming rate, emergency rooms around the country are seeing more victims of abuse than ever before. How would you respond to each of the following?

- A victim of child abuse?
- Spousal abuse?
- Elder abuse?
- A victim of a drunk driver?
- A gang beating, stabbing or gunshot victim?
- Multiple victims of a motor vehicle accident?

4. During your pastoral care training, you have come alongside patients and/or residents in various situations. They are often lonely, powerless, and frightened. Take some time here to review your experiences, asking God to give you insights about your encounters. Then answer the following questions:

- Which patient or resident stands out most in your mind? Explain.
- With which patient or resident did you feel the most discomfort? Explain. What did you do about it?
- What have you learned about yourself in ministering to the patients or residents?
- What have you learned about God from these experiences?

Chapter Resources

Berkley, James D. *Called Into Crisis* (The Leadership Library Series, vol. 18). Dallas TX: Word, 1989.

Cisney, Jennifer S., and Kevin L. Ellers. *The First 48 Hours: Spiritual Caregivers as First Responders*. Nashville: Abingdon, 2009.

Collins, Gary R. *How to Be a People Helper*. Wheaton, IL: Tyndale House Pub., 1995.

Floyd, Scott. *Crisis Counseling: A Guide for Pastors and Professionals*. Grand Rapids, MI: Kregel Academic & Professional, 2008.

Hendricks, James E. *Crisis Intervention: Contemporary Issues for On-Site Interveners*. Springfield, IL: U.S.A.: Thomas, 1985.

Hoff, Lee Ann. *People in Crisis: Understanding and Helping*, 4th ed. San Francisco, CA: Jossey-Bass, 1995.

Kanel, Kristi. *A Guide to Crisis Intervention*. Pacific Grove: Brooks/Cole, 1999.

Lampman, Lisa Barnes, ed. *Helping a Neighbor in Crisis*. Wheaton, IL: Tyndale House Pub., 1997.

Matsakis, A. *I Can't Get Over It: A Handbook for Trauma Survivors*, 2nd edition. Oakland, CA: New Harbinger, 1996.

Mitchell, Jeffrey T., and H. L. P. Resnick. *Emergency Response To Crisis: A Crisis Intervention Guidebook for Emergency Service Personnel*. Bowie, MD: R.J. Brady, 1981.

Mitchell, Juliann Whetsell. *The Dynamics of Crisis Intervention: Loss As the Common Denominator*. Springfield, IL: C. C. Thomas, 1999.

Roberts, Barbara. *Helping Those Who Hurt: A Handbook for Caring and Crisis*. Colorado Springs, CO: NavPress, 2009.

Stone, Howard W. *Crisis Counseling*, 3rd edition (Creative Pastoral Care and Counseling). Philadelphia: Fortress, 2009.

Swihart, Judson J., and Gerald C. Richardson. *Counseling in Times of Crisis*. Dallas, TX: Word, 1995.

Switzer, David K. *Pastoral Care Emergencies*. Minneapolis, MN: Fortress, 2000.

Wright, H. Norman. *The New Guide to Crisis & Trauma Counseling: A Practical Guide for Ministers, Counselors and Lay Counselors*. Ventura, CA: Regal, 2003.

8

Boundaries for Effective Ministry

Earth has its boundaries,
but human stupidity is limitless.
— Gustave Flaubert (1821-1880), French novelist[1]

No servant can be in bondage to two masters.
For either he will hate one and love the other,
or else he will cling fast to one and scorn the other.
You cannot be bondservants both of God and of gold
— Jesus (Luke 16:13, WNT)

Well-established and maintained boundaries serve to guide and protect us in all areas of life and ministry. One illustration of viewing boundaries as an important line of protection is to look at our own skin. Our skin helps to keep out countless, ever present threats to our physical well-being. For example, this natural barrier keeps our body safe and protected from germs. When there is a break in the skin, such as when we get a cut, we become open to infection. Just as our body needs a barrier of skin for protection, as a pastoral caregiver we also need ministry barriers that protect us and our ministry.

Psychologist and Professor Archibald Hart believes that every person involved in counseling, which includes pastoral caregivers, walks on the edge of a virtual moral precipice. One wrong step and we are over the edge.[2] That is why it is important for us as pastoral caregivers to evaluate whether or not we have set appropriate personal and professional parameters for our ministry activities. As pastoral caregivers, we are often responsible for caring, exploring alternatives, listening to and praying for hurting individuals. However, we are not responsible for their entire emotional well-being. As pastoral caregivers, we must create some type of emotional, physical and moral line (boundary, fence, or limit) that we are committed to never cross with a patient or resident, family member, staff person, or another pastoral caregiver.

We may mean well in our pastoral caring, but the Bible clearly speaks of the dilemma we face when attempting to justify and rationalize our good intentions: "The human heart is the most deceitful of all things, and desperately wicked. Who really knows how bad it is?" (Jeremiah 17:9, NLT)

As pastoral caregivers, we need to think through and establish ministry boundaries that will help us to respond appropriately to people with whom we come in contact. In no area is this more important than in our interactions with members of the opposite gender. And remember: These ministry boundaries are meant to be there for our own self-control, not for controlling others.

This chapter is designed to be a general overview of some (it is not meant to be exhaustive) of the prudent boundaries we need to consider when involved in pastoral relationships. May God bless us as we establish ministry boundaries that will help preserve and enhance our ministry as pastoral caregivers.

Importance of Boundaries

Why do we need ministry boundaries? Here are two reasons we need them.

To Guard Against Harm to the People We Serve

We may have good intentions to help, but we must also be competent to help. Dr. Mark Lasser, a counselor and nationally recognized expert in the field of sexual addiction, asserts this claim: "The counselor stands responsible to guard the safety of the client and is culpable for not doing so, no matter how the client behaves."[3]

We need to guard against exploiting clients. We must not intentionally take advantage of our "power" and "authority" with their "weakness" and "vulnerability." Anne Katherine, counselor and therapist, gives this caution:

The therapist-client relationship mirrors other relationships where one person is in the position of mentor, steward, authority, employer, or parent to another. Those with power have certain responsibilities toward the people they serve, assist, teach, supervise, or lead. The person who has power carries an ethical mandate not to exploit their position, not to abuse a subordinate in order to extract personal gain.[4]

We need to resist "rescuing" clients: doing for them what they are capable of doing for themselves. We need to avoid "going overboard" in our pastoral caregiving. We must not go beyond what is appropriate while trying to help them. This includes steering clear of over-investing ourselves.

According to Ken Royer, pastoral counselor at Link Care Center in Fresno, California:

The ultimate goal of Christian counseling is to increase the client's dependence upon God, not man. Counselors can be tempted to assume responsibility for the outcome of the presenting dilemma. An over-responsible counselor can unknowingly cripple a client's growth by fostering an unhealthy dependence that resembles a parent-child relationship. Meeting every need and answering every request is also a sure way to burnout.[5]

We need to guard against our own neediness. We must avoid role reversal regarding support. "Counter-transference" is the counselor's feelings toward the client as a result of his or her own emotional needs and projections, and must be carefully guarded against.

We need to defend against distorted expectations of the client. We also need to avoid attempting to fix everything with simple solutions and quick advice.

To Safeguard Against Ruining Our Ministry

Thomas Fischer, consulting director of Ministry Health, LLC, wisely declares:

The combination of poor boundaries and a passionate calling from God is like giving an adolescent the car keys for the first time. At best, it's precarious. At worst, it's an accident waiting to happen. The crash can be devastating.[6]

Having boundaries will protect us and our ministry from the devastation that a moral failure will cause. So much can be lost even through an accidental or well-intentioned act that is viewed as a violation of a boundary. For example, one pastoral caregiver regularly hugged people as a demonstration of his love for them. But when it comes to sexual harassment issues, it's not about our intent that matters but rather the perception of the recipient of our behavior. This pastoral caregiver was asked to no longer serve at the facility because his hugging was unwelcomed by one female colleague and it was therefore seen as inappropriate conduct (sexual harassment).

Remember Joseph and Potiphar's wife? We need to ask God regularly to preserve us from such a trial.

Confidentiality

Have we established guidelines to ensure that confidential communication between us and our clients remains private?

Definition: Keeping things confidential means that we do not pass on any communication revealed to us by a client in confidence to anyone else. Situations we know about are kept quiet, secure and private. Confidential client information includes all verbal, written, telephonic, or electronic communications arising within the helping relationship.

Doing anything beyond simple spiritual assessment and support requires the fully informed and uncoerced consent of the client. For example, initiating prayer with a client should take place only when the pastoral caregiver knows beyond any doubt that the person would welcome such a suggestion. Likewise, before discussing a client's case with his/her clergy or others, the pastoral caregiver must first obtain consent from the client.

If asked by legal counsel for confidential information about a client, then we respond with, "I *assert privilege* (a legal term) on that matter." That means no information about a client is to be shared even in a court of law.

Exceptions include:

- The client (and all parties involved) signs a release.
- The client demonstrates deadly harm to self and/or others (such as elder or child abuse). Such confessions require mandatory disclosure to the proper authorities, even in a clergy-client counseling context. Examples would include: the threat is serious and/or the client seems serious, the threat is imminent, the threat is doable, and the threat is an identifiable person.
- Minors. Anything a child says under the age of fifteen we may tell the parents. We need to remember to get written permission from the parents in order to counsel a minor (anyone under 18 years of age). Make sure to check the rules in your area, for the definition of a minor under different circumstances (for example, sexual activity) may vary from state to state.

Spiritual Boundaries

The spiritual aspect of our lives is never simply a *part* of life. Rather, it is at the *heart* and *center* of life. What spiritual disciplines have we established to advance our spiritual growth and to help guard against our crossing over our boundaries?

Spiritual Formation

We need to hear from God daily. Spending time in God's Word needs to be a priority in our ministry activities. Look at the example of Moses and Joshua in Exodus 33:11. In other words, we should not counsel others unless we have first had personal counsel from God.

Our effectiveness as a pastoral caregiver is directly and proportionately connected to our relationship with the Lord Jesus Christ. We need to put personal devotional time (worship, prayer, liturgy, meditation, quiet-time, etc.) at the top of our daily "to do" list.

Spiritual Abuse (Proselytizing)

Imposing our faith on another person (proselytizing) is never appropriate behavior for a pastoral caregiver. Pastoral caregivers demonstrate respect and sensitivity for the cultural and religious values of those they serve and refrain from coercing their own values and beliefs on those served. Anything in the nature of manipulation, any exploiting of any weakness, any use of coercion, is spiritual abuse and not a part of true evangelism.

Servanthood versus Servitude[7]

Understanding the difference between servitude and servanthood may be helpful in further understanding our boundaries. Servitude is associated with slavery; servanthood incorporates the idea of voluntary commitment. The former has four negative problems; the latter involves four healthy aspects.

Servitude	**Servanthood**
Over-identification:	Empathy:
This is taking on the problems of others at the expense of losing our own identity. For example, we don't need to jump into the mud hole in order to get someone out of it.	This is feeling with another person while retaining good objectivity and maintaining our own identity.
Superficial sweetness and gushiness:	Genuineness:
This is covering up our true feelings of frustration. We don't have to be delighted when dinner with our spouse is interrupted by an urgent (not an emergency) call.	This is being our authentic self; consistently being in congruence with who we are.
Being manipulated:	Meeting needs, not wants:
This is allowing others to abuse our caregiving relationship. We are being manipulated when another person controls our behavior or plays on our emotions for selfish ends. We do not need to be a doormat that is unable to say no to unreasonable requests.	This is speaking the truth in love. If we seek to help others, we need to meet their needs (such as needing a balanced diet), not their wants (for example, only wanting sweets).
Begrudging care:	Intentionality:
This is complaining about caregiving relationships in which we are involved. Our resentment of the situation will block effective relating and caring.	This is choosing to be in a caregiving relationship, or getting out of it when that is the best option for all concerned.

Physical Boundaries

What physical limits have we put into effect between us and those we minister to as a pastoral caregiver?

Obviously, there should be no sexual contact/touching. There is absolutely no room or place for such behavior. It is always a serious boundary violation.

Clearly, any sexual misconduct is unacceptable for a pastoral caregiver. This would include, but not be limited to, the solicitation of sexual or romantic relations, sexual harassment by comments, touch, or promises/threats of special action, seductive sexual speech or non-verbal behavior, nudity, innuendos, or "off-color" jokes.

This will bring up the question: "When is touching okay (for example, hugging)?" Here are some guidelines we will want to consider.

It's better to err on the safe side and not hug at all. Misplaced hugs have torn apart families and ruined lives. If you do decide to hug, avoid full-on, frontal hugs. Frontal hugs between a man and woman who are not related to each other are considered inappropriate in many cultures. Any hug that includes contact with the breast area is too intimate and therefore improper. Make it a one-armed or side-to-side hug and keep it brief. Don't let the hug last more than a second or two. A tight hug (big squeeze) is too intimate. A pat on the back is okay, but no rubbing. That's unacceptable. Always announce the hug and receive permission before doing it. "Hey! Come here; you need a hug. Is that okay?" Don't hug those you supervise.

In consideration of this topic, we will want to answer the following questions:

- How well do I know this person? Is there any emotional intimacy between the two of us? If so, be very careful with any physical contact.
- Is this person ready for a hug? If not, or we don't have permission, don't hug.
- How will this person and others interpret it? What message does a caring embrace send to another individual

who is looking to me for direction and purpose, but is also vulnerable to anyone with a caring touch? Again, it is the perception of others that matters, not our intent in giving the hug.

- Is it side-to-side (maybe okay) or frontal (usually not okay)?
- What if the person asks for a hug? It still may *not* be appropriate!
- Is our own marriage healthy? If not, refrain from contact with others and go give our spouse a meaningful hug.

According to Ken Royer, "We do not want to re-victimize a person who may have been abused."[8] That is another reason to use caution when giving a hug.

While we're on the subject of touching, what is the best way to hold someone's hand, like when we're praying with them? First of all, make sure we have their permission before we take their hand. Not everyone wants to hold hands. Second, once we have their permission to hold their hand, place our hand palm up when taking their hand. To place our hand palm down over their hand tends to project authority and indicate a dominant rather than submissive, non-threatening (palm up) role in the relationship. Interlocking fingers tends to communicate a deeper connection with each other.

Emotional/Social Boundaries

What emotional/social restrictions have we set up between ourselves and those we counsel? An "affair" is not usually a steamy, sexual experience. However, it is about accommodation, affirmation, adoration and affection.

A pastoral caregiver needs to refrain from counseling close, personal relationships. We will be prone to have a biased judgment with such people and the potential for client exploitation is a greater risk. Many dual relationships are wrong and indefensible (such as romantic or business relations, close friends or family members). The pastoral caregiver has the burden of proving a justified dual relationship by showing (1) informed consent, including discussion of how the counseling relationship might be harmed as other relations proceed, and (2) lack of harm or exploitation to the client.

We are to avoid "rescuing" (trying to fix) people (versus "helping" them).

We are never to rely on a client for personal support.

We must stay away from flirting. This should never occur in a pastoral care relationship. Giving compliments about appearance or giving long hugs or walking out with a colleague to their car can all be misunderstood by the recipient and viewed by others as flirting or sexual harassment.

Pastoral caregivers need to be careful with self-disclosure. We can ask ourselves, "Will what I say help *them* or *me*?" If it detracts from a focus on the client, then it is probably inappropriate. We should share only if we are convinced our comments will help solve the client's present problem and not distract the attention or diffuse the focus.

We will want to refrain from counseling someone of the opposite gender in a closed room or more than once. We can leave the door open or go to a room that has a window. Counseling (including mentoring and discipleship) is an intimate activity. And counseling the opposite sex is like playing with fire. We will probably want to limit the number of times we counsel someone of the opposite gender (once is best), and then refer him or her to another counselor.

We should avoid eating a meal alone with someone of the opposite gender. Sharing a meal together can be an intimate affair. Regardless of the innocence of our friendship, people can get the wrong idea if we are seen spending too much time together or are exclusive of others.

We will want to steer clear of riding alone in a car with someone of the opposite gender (other than a family member). That means no carpooling alone with someone of the opposite gender when going to a meeting or a visit. No lifts home for a nurse, doctor, babysitter, etc. We may see it as only trying to be helpful; they may perceive it as something more personal.

A pastoral caregiver should refrain from complimenting someone of the opposite gender about his or her coiffure, clothing, or physical appearance. Such references can be misinterpreted as romantic or sexual advances. Instead, compliment character and conduct. As pastoral caregivers, it is understandable that we want to be an encouragement to others. However, we should focus on things God is doing in a person's life (like their character) rather than the externals that can be easily misunderstood. Remember: Perception is everything. We might intend it as simply a compliment; however, they may perceive it as flirting.

We must avoid "toxic" humor. When people in positions of power or influence mistake degradation for comedy, the wound spreads wider than the immediate audience. Here are some guidelines for humor in the workplace[9]:

- If it's not language we would use with our mother or child, then don't use it with others in public.
- Make irony directed towards ourselves or our own situation.
- Avoid the use of sarcasm since the intent and impact are often wounding.
- Stories or "jokes" in which the subject or objects are people of different racial, ethnic, religious, gender, or sexual orientation than ourselves, are never appropriate in public, no matter how well we think we know the listener(s). Racist, sexist, and ageist comments are never appropriate, clever, or funny anywhere.
- Stories or "jokes" targeting physical or mental conditions are never appropriate anywhere.
- Stories or "jokes" about patients or residents are never appropriate without their express permission for the particular occasion.
- Stories or "jokes" about our colleagues should be saved for retirement "roasts," and then told with loving discretion. What we consider funny may not be to the colleague.
- Remember: the measure of appropriateness is the impact on others (in other words, their perception of the humor), not our intent.

Financial Boundaries

What monetary boundaries have we established for ourselves in relation to those we minister to, and especially within the healthcare setting?

We should discourage non-monetary compensation from clients (for example, having them do a favor for us or giving us a gift). Our church probably has a policy against such behavior (the hospitals definitely do), so abide by it.

A pastoral caregiver will want to pass up any kind of financial entanglement (such as borrowing or lending money).

We need to be very cautious when giving gifts (like at Christmas or for a birthday). It must be inexpensive and not of a personal nature (for example, jewelry or clothing). It would be a good idea for us to understand our answer to this question: What's my (or their) motivation/intent for giving the gift?

Additional Boundaries

Time Management

It is essential that we learn the concept of time-limited counseling sessions, phone calls, and visits. We need to be wise in allocating the time God has given us to care for people in need (Ephesians 5:15-16; Luke 4:42). Typical counseling sessions are not longer than fifty minutes. If more time is needed, reschedule another visit or refer them to someone who has the time and skill to help them.

Urgency versus Emergency

A pastoral caregiver needs to understand the difference between urgency and an emergency. *Urgency* is a situation where the person *wants* us to help him or her immediately. What they are requesting may be important (at least to them), but it is probably not necessary for us to immediately respond. If it can wait (and it usually can), postpone it. A real *emergency* is a situation where they definitely *need* us to help them right now.

Teamwork

We must learn to recognize and utilize teamwork. We need to understand our own counseling and knowledge limits. This is a boundary of humility. Understanding our limits will help us to make appropriate referrals to other clergy, social workers, and psychologists. No one is an expert in everything. Making a referral shows a healthy respect for the expertise of other professional caregivers.

Self Care

Pastoral caregivers need to exercise self-care and self-understanding. In the midst of so many demands and the temptation to meet their personal needs, what is appropriate self-care? Here are three areas to consider.[10]

Physical self-care. This would include stress management, exercising regularly, eating properly, getting enough rest, and having an annual physical by our family physician.

Mental self-care. Proverbs 23:7 reminds us that as we think in our heart, so are we. Mental self-care might include seeing a counselor or Pastor to check out how we perceive ourselves and our situation.

Emotional self-care. The Psalms are a primary emotional resource for us as ministers gifted with the capacity for feeling. A trained counselor or clergy person may also be able to help us sort out our sometimes conflicting feelings and guide us in ways to express or act on those feelings that are consistent with our values and responsibilities.

Ten Laws of Boundaries

Some of these "laws" have already been covered elsewhere, but it's worth summarizing these practical insights once again, which are from Dr. Cloud and Townsend.[11]

The law of *sowing and reaping*: Our actions certainly have consequences.

The law of *responsibility*: Boundaries help to determine who is responsible for what. We are responsible *to* one another, but not *for* each other. We are responsible for our own feelings, attitudes, values and handling of life's difficulties.

The law of *power*: We have power over some things (for example, influencing others, confessing our hurtful ways and repenting); we do not have power over other things (for example, we cannot change others).

The law of *respect*: If we wish for others to respect our boundaries, then we need to respect theirs.

The law of *motivation*: We must be free to say no before we can wholeheartedly say yes. Realize that when we say yes to one activity, we are also saying no to another. For example, when we say yes to an evening seminar, we are also saying no to spending time with our family that same evening.

The law of *evaluation*: We need to assess the pain our boundaries (or not having boundaries) might cause others. Sometimes that *pain* may lead to growth and sometimes it may lead to injury.

The law of *proactivity*: We take action to solve problems based on our values, wants and needs.

The law of *envy*: We will never get what we want if we focus outside our boundaries onto what others have. Envy is devaluing what we have, thinking it is not enough.

The law of *activity*: We need to take the initiative (rather than being passive and waiting for someone else to make the first move) in setting limits.

The law of *exposure*: We need to communicate our boundaries to each other.

Warning Signs

Those who have trespassed their boundaries have ignored some danger signs. Here are a few "red flags" and "flashing lights" that may indicate that we are about to or have already crossed a "no trespassing" line.

Having no accountability partner. We need someone else, preferably a peer, to objectively evaluate our ministry involvement and relationships on a regular basis.

Suffering persistent or increasing marital frustrations. Unhappiness in marriage will increase our vulnerability to temptation.

Undergoing excessive stress. The fatigue that comes from stress increases our vulnerability to temptation.

Experiencing chronic, low-level depression. This increases our vulnerability to temptation.

Going alone to breakfast, lunch, dinner, or social activities with a member of the opposite gender (other than our spouse). This should be a warning that your boundaries aren't working.

Dating or romantic involvement with a client. This one should have sirens going off as well as flashing red lights!

Changing normal office practices or routines. For example, if we are seeing someone away from the office, talking on the phone excessively or after hours with someone of the opposite gender, or sending e-mails or texting to someone of the opposite gender too often or after hours, this should be a warning sign that we have crossed a boundary.

Looking forward with unusual enthusiasm to a counseling session with someone of the opposite gender. This might be a good signal that it's time to make a referral.

Confiding in someone of the opposite gender. This should be done only with our spouse or accountability partner, never a client.

Relying on someone of the opposite gender for personal affirmation. Everyone needs personal "strokes." But to seek or expect such affirmation from a member of the opposite gender (other than our spouse) is a boundary violation that should not occur.

Asking or receiving very personal questions of someone of the opposite gender. This should be avoided. Yes, we need to be friendly. No, we don't need to be intimate.

Giving intimate, personal gifts to someone of the opposite gender or receiving personal gifts. Again, we need to avoid this kind of personal activity.

Thinking of a patient or resident as a friend rather than a client. A counselor is in danger of overstepping professional boundaries if s/he treats the client in a way that encourages personal friendship or becomes personally involved with the client or the client's problems. Such over-involvement will threaten to compromise objectivity, the development of transference (the client's projection onto the counselor of qualities of a significant other), and the counselor's ability to use the therapeutic relationship to help the client. We are there in the role of a pastoral caregiver, not as their "buddy."

Avoiding a Problem

The preceding "warning signs" are guidelines that will help us avoid most problems. In applying this advice to our lives, we will also want to consider the following:

Pray about our vulnerability. This invokes God's protection and increases our awareness of our vulnerability.

Develop a healthy fear of God. Since Proverbs 1:7 tells us that the fear of God is the "beginning of knowledge," this means that taking God into account in our daily lives is the foundation of a disciplined and holy life. To fear God means to adopt a godly lifestyle out of respect for Him. Consider the following passages: Joshua 24:14; 2 Kings 17:36, 39; Job 28:28; Psalm 34:7, 9; 85:9; Proverbs 8:13; 14:2, 16, 26-27; 19:23; Is 2:10, 19-21; 2 Corinthians 7:1; Hebrews 12:28-29; Revelation 14:7.

Intensify a super heightened awareness of the significant damage we will do to our ministry, marriage, family, church, friends, etc., if we crash through the barriers (even unintentionally) and fall over the edge. Consider the following passages: Proverbs 5:3-6; 7:1-27; 9:13-18.

We need to make our fences public. A boundary is useless if we can take it down any time our heart desires. Those around us (spouse, confidant, and colleagues) must understand our boundaries and be willing to tell us if they see one broken or becoming weak.

We should be accountable for the moral fences we have established. For example, we cannot trust ourselves to remain objective when it comes to sexuality. We need to be transparently accountable with a peer. No one understands the pressures on a minister as well as another minister. This person should be able to ask us straightforward questions like, "Have you set anything unclean before your eyes (Internet, TV, movies, and magazines) this week?" (See Psalm 101:3) And we need to give an honest answer. David is a good example of someone who attempted to rationalize his emotional vulnerability in having an affair with Bathsheba (2 Samuel 11:1-24). David needed an accountability partner (Nathan), and so do we.

Some of the objectives of an accountability group are:

To help clergy understand and accept their need for peer affirmation and for mutual accountability in personal life and in conducting public ministry, to offer clergy a place where they may temporarily set aside the role of "pastoral caregiver" and focus on their own care, health, and wholeness, to provide a safe place where clergy (or other leaders) can speak honestly about their personal or pastoral concerns and receive feedback in an informal and non-judgmental atmosphere, to reduce some of the intellectual, spiritual, and role-connected isolation experienced by many leaders.[12]

Pastoral caregivers must avoid sexual or romantic fantasies about their clients. This is one clear sign that we have lost control of our counter-transference. This would include looking forward with unusual enthusiasm to a counseling session with the person.

Recognize Satan's traps. Temptation can be subtle, but the payoff is not! Be on guard! As the Apostle Paul cautioned us: "So be careful. If you are thinking, 'Oh, I would never behave like that' — let this be a warning to you. For you too may fall into sin" (1 Corinthians 10:12, TLB).

Breaking major boundaries often happens over a gradual period of time. It is not a sudden blow out, but a slow leak. We may take small steps that subtly cross some minor boundaries without incident. These little infractions may eventually lead to crossing over some major boundaries. We might think, "I crossed the others without a problem, so there's no risk in crossing this one either." Do not believe that lie!

Correcting a Problem

What if we discover that we have transgressed (even unintentionally) any of our boundaries? What should we do?

First of all, stop seeing the client! Do this immediately—now, not later. *Refer* the client to someone else.

Then take a break from counseling. During the sabbatical, we need to take the time that is necessary to *rebuild* our fences.

Also consult with a professional counselor. We need to make every effort to *repair* our broken boundaries.

Finally, get ongoing supervision from a Pastor or counselor. We need to take time to regularly *reinforce* our fences through peer review.

Questions for Review

1. Why are boundaries important?
2. What does confidentiality mean?
3. What are some important spiritual boundaries?
4. Can you explain some emotional boundaries?
5. How would you explain teamwork as a boundary?
6. How is self-care a boundary?
7. How do you avoid a boundary problem?

Questions for Reflection

1. Spend several minutes in Bible study, reflection and prayer on 1 Corinthians 10:12-13. Record your insights in a journal and discuss your insights with a confidant and/ or the training team.
2. Read the following passages: Proverbs 5:3-6; 7:1-27; 9:13-18. After spending several minutes in Bible study, reflection and prayer about the consequences of stepping over moral boundaries, record your insights in a journal and share them with a confidant and/or the training team.

3. Jesus had boundaries for His life. He took time for solitude and He sought the company of friends. He got the sleep He needed, He ate healthy foods, and He did a lot of walking. He was never in a hurry or forced things to happen; yet He was committed to His mission. He said no to inappropriate behavior (the demands of the crowds, the lure of entitlement, the baiting questions, cynicism and pride). Find Bible verses for each of these examples of healthy boundaries. How do these apply to your own life? Discuss your insights with a confidant and/or the training team.

4. Jesus taught us about boundaries. For example, He instructed us about our personal prayer time (Matthew 6:6), about being honest and direct (Matthew 5:37), about setting priorities (Luke 16:13), about pleasing God and not people (John 5:44), and about obeying God (Matthew 21:28-31). In what ways does Christ's example and teaching about limits influence your own boundaries for your ministry? Share your insights with a confidant and/or the training team.

5. Knowledge is not enough. It is good to know about boundary guidelines. But it is not enough! Most who break through their moral fences clearly see the posted "NO TRESPASSING" signs. They know the boundaries, but deliberately choose to ignore them. Others naively cross boundaries when they confuse personal boundaries with professional boundaries. What are you going to do to make certain that this does not happen to you? Discuss this with a confidant and/or the training team.

6. Do you have a person (in addition to your spouse) to whom you are regularly accountable? Who is this person and how often do you meet? What are the guidelines s/he uses for holding you accountable for your spiritual, mental, emotional and physical conduct? Share your insights with a confidant and/or the training team.

However, accountability is not enough. It is good to be involved in an accountability group. But it is not enough! Most people who breach their moral boundaries do so while they deliberately lie to their accountability partner. What are you going to do to make certain this does not happen to you?

Chapter Resources

Cloud, Henry, and John Townsend. *Boundaries: When to Say Yes, How to Say No to Take Control of Your Life*, Revised ed. Grand Rapids, MI: Zondervan, 1992.

Doehring, Carrie. *Taking Care: Monitoring Power Dynamics and Relations Boundaries in Pastoral Care and Counseling.* Nashville: Abingdon, 1995.

Harbaugh, Gary L., Rebecca Lee Brenneis, and Rodney R. Hutton. *Covenants & Care: Boundaries in Life, Faith, and Ministry.* Minneapolis, MN: Fortress, 1998.

Haugk, Kenneth C. *Christian Caregiving: A Way of Life.* Minneapolis, MN: Augsburg, 1984. See Chapter 9 on "Servanthood v. Servitude" as an interesting perspective on ministry boundaries.

Johnson, David, and Jeff Van Vonderen. *The Subtle Power of Spiritual Abuse: Recognizing & Escaping Spiritual Manipulation and False Spiritual Authority Within the Church*, Reprint ed. Ada, MI: Bethany House, 2005.

Katherine, Anne. *Where to Draw the Line: How to Set Healthy Boundaries Every Day.* New York: Fireside, 2000.

Lebacqz, Karen, and Joseph D. Driscoll, *Ethics and Spiritual Care: A Guide for Pastors, Chaplains and Spiritual Directors*, Nashville: Abingdon, 2000.

Linden, Anné. *Boundaries in Human Relationships: How to be Separate and Connected.* Bancyfelin: Crown House Pub., 2008.

London, H. B., Jr., Neil B. Wiseman, and Robert N. Hosask, eds. *Pastors at Risk: Help for Pastors, Hope for the Church.* Wheaton, IL: Victor, 1993.

Mosgofian, Peter, and George Ohlschlager. *Sexual Misconduct in Counseling & Ministry.* Nashville, TN: Word, 1995.

O'Neil, Mike S., and Charles E. Newbold, Jr. *Boundary Power: How I Treat You, How I Let You Treat Me, How I Treat Myself*, 2nd ed. Nashville: Sonlight, 1994.

Peterson, Marilyn R. *At Personal Risk: Boundary Violation in Professional-Client Relationships*. New York: Norton, 1992.

Poling, James Newton. *The Abuse of Power: A Theological Problem*. Nashville: Abingdon, 1991.

Ragsdale, Karen Hancock, editor. *Boundary Wars: Intimacy and Distance in Healing Relationships*. Cleveland, OH: Pilgrim, 1996.

Reediger, G. Lloyd. *Ministry and Sexuality: Cases, Counseling, and Care*. Minneapolis, MN: Fortress, 1990.

Wilson, Michael Todd, and Brad Hoffman. *Preventing Ministry Failure: A ShepherdCare Guide for Pastors, Ministers and Other Caregivers*. Downers Grove, IL: IVP, 2007.

9

Avoiding Compassion Fatigue: Balancing the Burdens of Caregiving

Burnout is nature's way of telling you, you've been going through the motions your soul has departed; You're a zombie, a member of the walking dead, a sleepwalker.
— Sam Keen, American author, professor, philosopher[1]

Come to me, all of you who are weary and carry heavy burdens, and I will give you rest.
— Jesus (Matthew 11:28, NLT)

Understanding Burnout/Compassion Fatigue: Comprehending the Burden

Definition of Burnout and Compassion Fatigue

*B*urnout Definition: Psychologist Herbert Freudenberger, who claims credit for the term, explains burnout as depleting oneself; exhausting one's physical and mental resources; and wearing oneself out by excessively striving to reach some unrealistic expectation imposed by oneself or by the values of society.[2] Christina Maslach, a psychologist and early researcher of the problem, defined burnout as "a syndrome of emotional exhaustion, depersonalization, and reduced personal accomplishment that can occur among individuals who do 'people work' of some kind."[3]

The word, as explained in Webster's New International Dictionary, has three meaningful examples for its use:

The burning out of the interior or contents of something, such as a building. We can probably visualize ourselves being devoured from within by our fiery expenditure of energy for doing ministry until we have nothing left.

The breakdown of an electrical circuit owing to combustion caused by high temperatures. In this case, the high temperature produced by the electrical current burns out a conductor. In application to ourselves in ministry, our emotional energy supply can become completely short-circuited due to the over-heating of the constant stress of ministry activity.

The severe denuding of the forest floor as a result of a forest fire. Our resources to rejuvenate ourselves may become utterly consumed by the stressful burdens we endure so that renewal seems hopelessly difficult.

More specifically, burnout is associated with lots of sources of stress and hassles involved with our work (tensions with supervisors, work schedules, co-workers, paper work, equipment malfunctions, the bureaucratic system, etc.). It is a state of extreme dissatisfaction with our work as we work too long, too hard and under too much pressure. Burnout results in a loss of enthusiasm, energy, idealism, perspective and purpose on a mental, physical, emotional and spiritual level.

Burnout for pastoral caregivers can happen when we become extremely dissatisfied with our ministry and become cynical, depressed, emotionally exhausted, irritable with team members, and even impaired. Burnout requires professional help and we should discontinue being a caregiver until the cynicism and impairment are gone.

Compassion Fatigue Definition: Compassion Fatigue is the notion of being burned out by the kind of ministry that we do, the kind of patients and families that we deal with and the residue from ministering to those hurting people. It is not about problems and hassles at work, but it is about the stress associated with the clients we deal with in ministry. It represents the cost of caring about and for seriously ill patients and residents and their families. It is the emotional residue of exposure to coming alongside the suffering. It is the compassion-consuming calling of being a pastoral caregiver to seriously ill people.

Compassion fatigue happens when caregivers (people helpers like you) become emotionally drained because of hearing about all of the pain and trauma of their clients and family members. The caregivers still care and want to help, but they no longer have the emotional energy to do so. Taking time off, getting professional help and nurturing ourselves can usually help us return to being healthy, helpful pastoral caregivers.

Symptoms of Burnout

Physical Indications of Burnout
- A persistent sense of physical fatigue: feeling "run down" and exhausted and "keeping up to speed" becomes increasingly difficult.
- Frequent headaches, migraines.
- Chronic muscle tensions, especially of the head, neck and/or lower back.
- Gastrointestinal problems (ulcers).
- Decreased appetite (or a never-satisfied appetite).
- Sleeplessness in spite of feeling fatigued.
- High blood pressure.
- Shortness of breath.
- Nervous tics, tremors, teeth/jaw clenching.

Psychological Indications of Burnout
- Depression ("I don't care anymore!").
- A dulling affect, mental fatigue ("I can't think straight anymore!").
- Increased irritability, hostility ("I hate this job now!").

- Decreased tolerance for frustration ("I can't take it anymore!").
- Feelings of helplessness, an inability to see a way out of problems ("Every day I dread going to work!").
- Increased risk taking and impulsivity ("Let's just do it!").
- Inflexibility of behavior and goals ("I can't adjust to this anymore!").
- Cynicism and negativism about self, others, work and the world in general ("I can't stand this anymore!").
- Apathy ("I don't care anymore!").
- Reduction and/or abandonment of recreational activities ("I'd rather stay home now!").
- Decreased capacity for pleasure and social contacts ("I don't want to go out anymore!").
- Withdrawal, detachment ("I'd rather be alone!").
- Increased interpersonal and/or marital discord ("I'm having trouble getting along with my spouse!").

Spiritual Indications of Burnout
- Disillusionment and disappointment with God. We feel that God is powerless to help ("What can He do?"). We feel that God doesn't care ("What does He care?"). We feel that God has abandoned us, our clients, and the families ("Where is He?").
- Discontinuance of religious practices. We stop worshipping—privately and corporately ("I don't feel like going to church anymore!"). We stop praying ("I don't feel like praying!"). We stop reading the Bible (I don't feel like reading my Bible!").
- Development of spiritual apathy ("I don't care anymore!").

Performance Indications of Burnout
- Decreased efficiency.
- Diminished initiative.
- Reduced interest in work (as well as a general apathy).
- Depleted ability to work under stress.
- Difficulty concentrating or paying attention.
- Increased irritation with colleagues.

- Increased use of tranquilizers, alcohol, cigarettes.

Causes of Burnout and Compassion Fatigue

The personality traits of the individual who is likely to develop burnout may embrace some of the following characteristics:

- Someone highly task and goal oriented.
- A person who takes particular satisfaction in doing things neat and orderly (a perfectionist).
- Someone with a high need for achieving "control" of self, others and/or the environment; is intensely competitive.
- An individual who tends to be overly critical but cannot stand criticism.
- Someone with a marked capacity to delay gratification (or perhaps an inability to allow personal satisfaction).
- A person with very high personal expectations and exaggerated expectations of others.
- Someone whose work and "productive" activity is over-valued and provides the major source of self-esteem and pleasure. *Doing* is the key to being worthwhile.
- An individual with a scarcity of non-work related interests, such as recreation and hobbies.

How many of these characteristics are consistent with most people involved in ministry? In what ways do *you*, as a pastoral caregiver, indentify with these traits, especially as you take a close look at your own life and lifestyle?

The people who are most prone to compassion fatigue are:

- Those who minister to people who are in need, who are hurting, who have special problems going on in their lives and who have significant health issues; therefore, the pastoral caregiver is basically vulnerable to being overwhelmed by their experience as they absorb the trauma through their eyes and ears.
- Those who are deeply sensitive, who care a lot about their clients, who are willing to work the extra time, who are

willing to put more into their ministry than they put into almost any other aspect of their lives, who tend to identify with the clients and families, and who do a poor job of replenishing themselves physically, emotionally and spiritually.

This means we, as pastoral caregivers, are vulnerable to experiencing compassion fatigue.

Warning Signs of Burnout and Compassion Fatigue

Just as meteorologists can recognize certain warning signs of an approaching storm, so psychologists can recognize symptoms of approaching burnout. As Freudenberger notes, they involve the following characteristics[4]:

Exhaustion. A lack of energy associated with feelings of tiredness and trouble keeping up with one's usual activities.

Detachment. Putting distance between oneself and other people, particularly those with whom we have close relationships.

Boredom and Cynicism. We begin to question the value of friendships and activities—even of life itself.

Increased Impatience and Irritability. As burnout takes hold, our ability to accomplish things diminishes and our impatience grows and causes flare-ups with others.

A Sense of Omnipotence. We have thoughts such as: "Nobody can do my job better than I can."

Feelings of Being Unappreciated. Burnout victims experience complex feelings of bitterness, anger and resentment for not being appreciated more for their added efforts.

Change of Work-Style. Reduced results and conflicts with colleagues will eventually cause us either to withdraw from decisive leadership and work habits, or to seek to compensate for the conflicts by becoming more tyrannical, demanding and inflexible.

Paranoia. Once burnout has taken a long-term hold, it's a small step from feeling unappreciated to feeling mistreated and threatened.

Disorientation. Long-term burnout increases difficulty with wandering thought processes.

Psychosomatic Complaints. Headaches, lingering colds, backaches, and similar complaints are often a result of the burnout victim's emotional stress.

Depression. In burnout, the depression is usually temporary, specific and localized, pertaining more or less to one area of our life.

Major Depression. This state is usually prolonged and pervades all areas of our lives.

Suicidal Thinking. As the depression progresses, the result can be suicidal thoughts: "Life isn't worth living anymore!"

We need to ask ourselves, "Am I experiencing any of these warning signs in my life?" If we are, what are we going to do about it?

Implications of Burnout and Compassion Fatigue

When I was a teenager, I worked at a rustic church camp that only had hot water for showers if it was heated by a furnace. A fire was built in the furnace, which heated the water running through pipes in the upper part of the furnace, and then the hot water collected in a holding tank before going to the showers. There was no pressure release valve on the holding tank. The shower heads were the pressure release valve. One day nobody took any showers after a fire had been built in the furnace. Soon the water turned to steam and the steam had no place to go. The holding tank couldn't take the pressure any longer and the bottom blew out of it.

The implication (application) for our lives: Without a "pressure release valve" for our lives, the pressure can build to dangerous levels. We need to ask ourselves: "Can I feel the strain of the pressure building up inside me from my pastoral caregiving?" If so, when and how will we "release" the pressure before we "explode"?

Rechargeable batteries are a wonderful tool. But if they are constantly being used without recharging them, they will eventually use up their power and become useless.

The application for our lives is quite evident: Without "recharging the battery" of our souls after continuous use in ministry, we will surely become powerless and useless. As we think about it, can we sense that we are running low on physical, emotional and spiritual energy? If so, when and in what ways will we "recharge" ourselves?

An automobile will serve us well as long as it is well maintained. Because a car is valuable, we tend to invest in maintaining it. However, if we never do any routine maintenance on the car (like changing the oil), we can do some serious damage to the engine and it can eventually fail to operate altogether.

Consider the application to our involvement in ministry: Can we feel the wear and tear of the many miles our body has experienced in serving others? If so, and because we are valuable, when and how are we going to schedule some routine "maintenance" on our lives?

I thoroughly enjoy backpacking in the mountains. This is a wonderful experience as long as we don't overload the pack and keep it balanced. I was with an inexperienced backpacker once who tried taking too much weight and also had the backpack load unbalanced so that it rubbed on one hip. It resulted in some serious wear and tear on the body that required some special attention to bandage the hip where the skin was rubbed raw.

Here is the application for our lives: "Overloading the system" can inevitably lead to a serious breakdown. As a pastoral caregiver, can we feel the weight bearing down upon us, overloading our physical, emotional and spiritual systems? If so, when and in what ways are we going to "lighten" (and balance) the load?

Resolving Burnout/Compassion Fatigue: Countering the Burden

Example from the Old Testament

Let's examine an Old Testament example from the life of Elijah (1 Kings 18—19). This example begins with the aggravation that leads to the burnout. Burnout frequently occurs after intense "peak" experiences, such as Elijah's "mountain top" victory (1 Kings 18). Elijah had recently experienced the greatest success of his career: the ending of a famine, a revival among the people, the priests of Baal eliminated, and his credibility restored. Then he experiences despondency, which can often follow prolonged intensity (1 Kings 19). Elijah demonstrates a classic example of Frudenberger's description:

> *It's the letdown that comes in between crises or directly after "mission accomplished." Frequently, following a triumph, high achievers (Elijah certainly qualifies) suffer periods of deep melancholia akin to the postpartum depression some women experience after giving birth. The feelings are remarkably similar: sadness, separation, sluggishness, and above all, emptiness.*[5]

Other stress-related characteristics Elijah exhibited during his burnout were:

- Rejection (v. 2).
- Detachment (he ran away from everyone, v. 3).
- Exhaustion (physically, v. 5-6, mentally, emotionally and spiritually).
- Suicidal thoughts (an advanced stage of the depression and despair that result from burnout, v. 4).
- Bitterness (he reminded God how zealous he had been, v. 10).
- Feelings of being indispensable (v. 10).
- Feelings of being mistreated (v. 10).
- Feelings of self-pity (v. 10).
- Feelings of persecution (he felt put upon and became increasingly suspicious of those around him).

Next comes the adaptation to the stressful situation. We can learn much from what God did to minister to His servant's physical, emotional and spiritual needs during this time of compassion fatigue. Therapy came in the form of God's presence, His loving patience, and His purposeful assignment. And Elijah was fully restored by God's intervention! Look at what happened:

- God provided time for sufficient rest and proper nourishment (v. 5-6).

- God offered a "quiet time" for Elijah (v. 12).
- God provided a sense of companionship (v. 18).
- God gave him an assignment that he was capable of fulfilling (v. 16).

Finally, there is the application of this example for our personal lives. Opening ourselves to God, our personal Counselor and Comforter, can also change our perspective of the pressure. He does understand what we are going through. Hear His words of comfort through the pen of the Psalmist:

> *In my anguish I cried to the LORD,*
> *and He answered by setting me free.*
> *The LORD is with me; I will not be afraid.*
> *What can man do to me?*
> *The LORD is with me; He is my helper.*
> *I will look in triumph on my enemies.*
> *It is better to take refuge in the LORD*
> *than to trust in man.*
> *It is better to take refuge in the LORD*
> *than to trust in princes.* (Psalm 118:5-9)

Example from the New Testament

Let's look at a New Testament example from the life of Jesus (Mark 6:7, 12-13, 30-32).

Jesus recognized that the stresses of life can lead to physical, emotional and spiritual symptoms of burnout. He also recognized that these stress levels needed to be lightened so that recovery can begin. It is relatively easy to become so concerned with "getting the job done" that we lose sight of the needs of the people who are actually carrying out the work. A close examination of His brief statement shows there are three key elements that can relieve the stresses that lead to burnout:

1. A change in *location* to experience peace and quiet.
2. A change in activity or responsibility—to rest up while doing something different.

3. A certain amount of *time* to take a break for a planned amount of time.

In applying this example to our own lives, consider the following:

- Know our own "triggers" and vulnerable areas and learn to defuse them or avoid them.
- Resolve our personal issues and continue to monitor our reactions to other's pain.
- Be human and allow ourselves to grieve when bad things happen to us and others.
- Develop realistic expectations about the rewards as well as limitations of being a people helper.
- Set and follow appropriate limits and boundaries for ourselves and tell them to others.

Physical Renewal

We can experience physical renewal **through exertion**. Because ministry can be a sedentary vocation, we need to adopt a thirty to sixty minute program of regular (at least three hours per week) physical activity—in the form of jogging, walking, bicycling, swimming, tennis, racquetball, jazzercise, basketball, working out at the local gym—anything, as long as we find the exercise interesting (so we will keep at it) and it is strenuous enough to produce deep breathing and liberal perspiration (so our body benefits from it).

We need to consult with our physician for a recommendation of a safe level of exercise for what is right for us—especially if we are over forty years old or have any health conditions or medical complications.

Another way we can renew ourselves physically is **through nutrition**. We need to regularly eat a well-balanced diet when under a lot of pressure. Most nutritionists agree that the best diet is a balanced one that includes some portions from all of the food groups in the food pyramid.

There are some foods we might want to limit when experiencing stress. Reduce the amount of caffeine-rich beverages consumed (especially coffee, colas, and tea). Decrease the intake of fat and sugar. It has been said that, "Our reserves in physical energy disappear proportionately as our waistline expands."

We also need to get enough fluids into our system throughout each day. Why? Dehydration causes stress in our body. The universal recommendation is six to eight glasses of water a day.

We can obviously renew our physical energy *through relaxation*. To sleep soundly for a full night is a valuable restorative gift. Proper rest allows our physical, mental and emotional self to regain lost energy. Rest restores us! Each of us needs to determine how much sleep we need to feel and function at our best and then we need to determine to get it most nights during the week.[6]

We need to take appropriate breaks daily—not working for too long a period of time and not working in one situation for too long. We need weekly breaks—not working over fifty hours a week—which means we need time off on the weekend from ministry activity. We need to take a quarterly long weekend off and a yearly break of at least two weeks off.

Finally, we can enjoy physical renewal *through avoiding addiction*. We must avoid using drugs and alcohol to help us cope with stress. Tranquilizers and sleeping pills should be used only under a doctor's care and with extreme caution. Drugs and alcohol merely numb the symptoms of stress. They do nothing to help cure the cause. In fact, alcohol can actually *cause* stress. In laboratory tests, alcohol was shown to trigger the release of stress hormones from the brain and pituitary and adrenal glands—the same reaction that can be brought on by money woes or marital problems.

Emotional Renewal

One way to experience emotional renewal is *though talking with a friend*. A common ingredient among people who experience burnout is the fact that they do not have a friend to whom they are close enough to share their personal feelings and still feel loved and accepted. Studies show that people with social networks handle crises better. We need to cultivate a confidant with whom we can openly and honestly discuss what is going on in our heart and mind. The very worst way to deal with burnout is to bury it inside. The lack of a feedback system is not a sign of strength, but a sign of being foolish. We need someone to listen attentively while we share our concerns and heartaches and who can honestly respond to us with supportive comfort and counsel. Regularly discussing our frustrations and fears with someone we trust can provide substantial relief from pressure—even if it seems that at times nothing at all can help. Simply being able to put words to our feelings in the presence of a supportive person can be very freeing—it can even reenergize us.

Another way to experience emotional renewal is *through laughing*. A wise man once compared a cheerful heart to good medicine (Proverbs 17:22). Humor, if we use it well, can be one of the most helpful things we can do to relieve tension. Being able to laugh about something often helps us to put it into proper perspective. Answer this question: "Have I laughed several times today?" If not, then we need to do something to make us laugh: read a joke book, watch a comedy, look at old photos, whatever, as long as it will make us smile. Enjoy life!

We can surely find emotional renewal *through support*. We need to find opportunities to acknowledge, express and work through our experiences in a supportive environment. Seek assistance from other colleagues and caregivers who have worked in a similar environment and have remained healthy and hopeful. We need to develop a healthy support system to protect ourselves from compassion fatigue and the emotional exhaustion that comes with it.

Emotional renewal doesn't only happen by being with other people, it can also occur when we are by ourselves. One way this can happen is *through journal writing*. Personal journal writing is a consummate prescription for self-discovery, problem solving and healing emotional wounds. Our inner world may be clarified, calmed and comforted by revealing our feelings on paper (or a computer). If we are one of those who have never kept a journal before, we will want to do some research on helpful hints about how to get started.[8]

Spiritual Renewal

Our spirituality—our sense of belonging to God completely and of God's abundant life in us—is, in the opinion of many, the most important element in coping with stress in our life. And Dr. Frederic Flach agrees: "I believe the most vital ingredient of resilience is faith."[7] In the words of David A. Ruch, M.Div., M.A., and a licensed clinical professional counselor:

> *Our limitations as healers should draw us constantly back to dependency on God not only for power and faith to continue but for comfort and perspective when we feel defeated. When we recalibrate ourselves based on His sovereignty rather than our circumstances, we have new hope.*[9]

One way we can obviously experience spiritual renewal is **through adoration**. There is something uplifting and rejuvenating from spending time in praise and worship with a group of people who share our beliefs. And Scripture encourages us to not avoid it (Hebrews 10:25).

There is therapeutic power for physical, emotional and spiritual renewal in listening to and singing inspirational music. For example, a hymn based on an early Greek hymn that dates as far back as the eighth century can encourage us with these words:

> *Art thou weary, art thou languid,*
> *   Art thou sore distressed?*
> *"Come to me," saith One, "And coming*
> *   Be at rest."*
> *Hath He marks to lead me to Him*
> *   If He be my Guide?*
> *In His feet and hands are wound-prints,*
> *   And His side.*
> *Finding, following, keeping, struggling,*
> *   Is He sure to bless?*
> *Saints, apostles, prophets, martyrs,*
> *   Answer, "Yes."*[10]

When pressing situations are upon us, we need to take time out to get spiritually oriented in order to refocus our attention on the "Problem Solver" who is greater than any of our pressures. Worship is one way to experience a rejuvenating supply of wisdom and strength and peace from God. We need to come to Him and unload our cares (Psalm 55:22; 1 Peter 5:7). He can handle it.

Another way to experience spiritual renewal is *through education*. Read an inspirational book. We need to stimulate our soul as we gain understanding, find encouragement, and revitalize our hope through the experiences and lessons of others. Especially consider reading a biography of a missionary. These folks faced many trials with faith and courage and their lives are an inspirational testimony for us today.

Read a devotional book. We can become acquainted with our spiritual source of hope and renew our faith through the reading of the Scriptures associated with our belief system. Meditating on the Word of God allows God to speak to us personally through the words that apply, in one way or another, to all believers. I find the words in Isaiah 40:27-31 or Lamentations 3:1-26 or Matthew 11:28-30 especially good to read when I am feeling weary and faint from the burdens pressing down upon me. We can experience hope and renewal when our attention is focused beyond our circumstances to the all-sufficient character of the eternal, faithful, all-powerful, ever-present, gracious Creator.

We can certainly experience spiritual renewal *through meditation*. Prayer is the spontaneous, heartfelt sharing by needy human beings with God, who is able and willing to help. Bringing our pressures to God can change our perspective—it can keep us from becoming myopic—and help us to cope. Through prayer and meditation we can sweep the mind of all turmoil. In place of our exhaustion and spiritual fatigue, God will give us rest and shalom. All He asks is that we spend time with Him, meditating on Him, talking to Him, listening in silence, occupying ourselves with Him (Hebrews 12:3).

An additional way we can experience spiritual renewal is *through absolution*. We need to practice confession. Ignoring transgression (when we have "crossed the line") in our life will tend to place a great emotional, spiritual and physical burden on our life (Psalm 32:3-4). God's forgiveness is always sufficient and immediately available (1 John 1:9). He welcomes repentance with open arms.

We need to practice forgiveness (Colossians 3:13; Ephesians 4:31-32). If we do not forgive others, we will tend to turn our anger inward, which results in bitterness and depression, and we will experience burnout symptoms. In an interview by Piers Morgan with Rick and Kay Warren regarding the death of their son, Rick Warren said,

> *I forgive, first, because I've been forgiven by God. Second, unforgiveness makes me miserable. And third, I'm going to need more forgiveness in the future. So we don't forgive for their benefit. We actually forgive for ours.*[11]

Forgiveness involves an act of the will—it is choosing to no longer hold a grudge against an offending party. Freedom from bitterness (through forgiveness) is necessary for effective recovery from burnout and for avoiding it in the first place.

Diversional Renewal

If we are going to renew ourselves from the stresses of life, we need diversions from the normal hectic pace. We need to practice diversional renewal ***through relaxation*** techniques.

Maintaining good mental health often involves learning to relax. There are many books, audios and seminars that can help teach us personal techniques on learning to mentally and physically relax. When the sympathetic nervous system is quieted by these practices, muscle tension decreases, heart rate slows, and a sense of well-being is achieved.

Here is one progressive muscle relaxation method for you to try. Isolate yourself from all noises and distractions (like the phone, TV, etc.). Sit in a comfortable chair with your feet flat on the floor (or, if you are in a recliner chair, resting comfortably on the footrest). Have your hands resting comfortably in your lap or upon the armrests. Close your eyes. Make a deliberate effort to relax all your muscles. Sometimes this is best achieved by first flexing the muscles and then letting them relax. Begin with your head, then relax all your neck and back muscles. Let your chest and stomach muscles release their tension. Feel your arms becoming limp. Allow your legs and feet to completely relax. Spend about ten to fifteen minutes relaxing all your muscles as you feel the tension drain from your body.

Another way to experience renewal through diversion is *through recreation*. We need to have a life beyond our professional work and ministry that nurtures us personally. Leisure is free activity, whereas labor is compulsory activity. In leisure we do what we like, but in labor we do what we must. In our labor we meet the objective needs and demands of others, but in leisure we scratch the subjective itches within ourselves. Some recommend engaging in some form of enjoyable recreation (leisure time) at least three times per week—something not connected with our usual line of work. Watching make-believe characters on TV is never a substitute for experiencing life for ourselves.

Take Mini-Vacations. If we are "vacating" only once a year (like many people), that block of time almost suffocates in the desperate attempt to cram a whole year's worth of happy escape into two weeks. We would fare much better to plan more consistent and more frequent breaks, each with a different purpose, to meet the various needs of our family. We need to break the habit of looking to the TV for our happiness each weekend. During our lunch break (a respite time) we might include: going on a picnic, working on a puzzle, going for a walk around the block, buying some flowers for the desk, or reading from a good book. After dinner we might get involved in: playing a table game, singing a song together as a family, doing finger painting together, going swinging in the park, or watching the sunset from a hill top.

Organizational Renewal

Through position—our priorities. We need to ask ourselves: "What are my priorities?" We need to try and keep a firm rein on our priorities, especially at times of greatest anticipated stress.

We are likely to be an over-estimator as to what we can realistically do. We probably find it difficult to say "No"—both to ourselves and to others who may place demands on us. We must be rigorous in our assessment of priorities concerning meeting the needs of others. We need to practice saying no to activities of lesser priority—regardless of how worthwhile they may seem. Think about the idea that if we never say "no", what is our "yes" worth?

Set and keep healthy boundaries for work. We need to ask ourselves, "Will the world fall apart if I step away from my ministry for a day (or a week)?"

Through intentions—our plans. Don't take self-care for granted. We must plan for it. Answer this question: "Do I have a plan for using my time wisely?" Organizing our life may appear like a tall order with which we have difficulty at times, but we can learn to plan ahead. When we know what needs to be done, we are not as prone to experience surprises in our life. If emergencies do arise, then it tends to be easier to cope with them. While it is not necessary to become a slave to a schedule, getting organized can help us run our life more smoothly and efficiently.

Part of organizing our life involves planning "time outs" or mini-vacations. This is necessary for our survival. We need to consider creating small "buffer zones" between some of our obligations to allow ourselves ten to fifteen minutes to close our eyes, pray, listen to music, relax, reorient our priorities, and defuse our tension.

Time can work for or against us, depending on how we choose to use it. We can allow ourselves to procrastinate and then rush to meet deadlines. We can leave little time to finish projects and work under that pressure. We can hurry from one activity to another without taking a moment to catch our breath or utter a prayer. But when we organize our time, by setting priorities and planning accordingly, we stay directed and live a purposeful life that is much less stress-filled.

May you find God's "rest" even as you work hard at coming alongside the hurting (see Hebrews 4:9-11).

Questions for Review

1. How do you define compassion fatigue?
2. What is one thing you can do for physical renewal?
3. How can you achieve emotional renewal?
4. What can you do to experience spiritual renewal?
5. How will diversional renewal work for you?
6. What will organizational renewal look like for you?

Questions for Reflection

1. Take the Professional Quality of Life Scale (ProQOL 5) test and discuss with a confidant and/or the training team. Get the test and self-score it by going online at: www.proqol.org/ProQol_Test.html.
2. Read Luke 10:38-42 as an example of "overload" in the life of Martha as contrasted with Mary. What are your "triggers" or vulnerable areas of stress (kinds of problems and challenges) that could cause you stress in coming alongside patients or residents and families? After spending several minutes in Bible study, reflection and prayer about the overload in your own life, complete a personal plan for avoiding compassion fatigue and then discuss this plan with a confidant and/or the training team.
3. It doesn't matter how much darkness there is around you, but how you stand in it is what really matters. What can you do to keep yourself healthy (physically, emotionally and spiritually well) as a caregiver in the midst of the "dark nights"? Share your insights with a confidant and/or the training team.

Chapter Resources

Berry, Carmen Renee. *When Helping You Is Hurting Me: Escaping the Messiah Trap.* San Francisco: Harper & Row, 1988.
Coleman, Lyman, and Marty Scales, eds. *Stress Management: Finding the Balance.* Littleton, CO: Serendipity House, 1992.

Demaray, Donald E. *Watch Out for Burnout: A Look at its Signs, Prevention, and Cure*. Grand Rapids, MI: Baker, 1983.

Ellison, Craig. *From Stress to Well-Being: Counseling to Overcome Stress*. Nashville: Thomas Nelson, 2002.

Farrar, Steve. *Overcoming Overload: Seven Ways to Find Rest in Your Chaotic World*. Colorado Springs, CO: Multnomah, 2004.

Faulkner, Brooks R. *Burnout in Ministry: How to Recognize it; How to Avoid it*. Nashville: Broadman, 1981.

Figley, Charles R. *Compassion Fatigue: The Stress of Caring Too Much*. Panama City, FL: Visionary Productions, 1994.

Freudenberger, Herbert J., and Geraldine Richelson. *Burnout: The High Cost of High Achievement*. New York: Bantam, 1981.

Holtz, Adam R. *Beating Busyness*. Colorado Springs, CO: NavPress, 1999.

Ilse, Sherokee. *Giving Care, Taking Care: Support for the Helpers*. Maple Plain, MN: Wintergreen, 1996.

Maslach, Christina. *Burnout: The Cost of Caring*. Cambridge, MA: Malor, 2003.

Miller, James E. *The Caregiver's Book: Caring for Another, Caring for Yourself*. Minneapolis, MN: Fortress, 1996.

Mills, Bill, and Craig Parro. *Battling Burnout in Ministry*. Palos Heights, IL: Leadership Resources International, 1997.

Minirth, Frank B., ed. *Beating Burnout: Balanced Living for Busy People*. New York: Inspirational, 1997.

Powell, Cliff, and Graham Barker. *Unloading the Overload: A Christian Guide to Managing Stress*. London: Gazelle, 1999.

Rassieur, Charles L. *Christian Renewal: Living Beyond Burnout*. Philadelphia: Westminster, 1984.

Sanford, John A. *Ministry Burnout*. New York: Paulist, 1982.

Sherman, James R. *Preventing Caregiver Burnout*. Golden Valley, MN: Pathway, 1994.

Swenson, Richard A. *Margin: Restoring Emotional, Physical, Financial, and Time Reserves to Overloaded Lives*. Colorado Springs, CO: NavPress, 2004.

Tan, Siang-Yang. *Rest: Experiencing God's Peace in a Restless World*. Vancouver: Regent College Pub., 2003.

Wilson, Michael Todd, and Brad Hoffman. *Preventing Ministry Failure: A ShepherdCare Guide for Pastors, Ministers and Other Caregivers*. Downers Grove, IL: IVP, 2007.

Chaplaincy Care and Clinical Pastoral Education

I think it's important to clarify a distinction between a Board Certified Chaplain (BCC) and other spiritual caregivers. There are many who use "spiritual care" and "pastoral care" synonymously with "chaplaincy services," while others see distinct differences between them. Let me explain my understanding, and the understanding of other professional chaplaincy organizations, of the differences between these terms.

Spiritual Care

First of all, *Spiritual Care* comes under the larger umbrella of basic spiritual support that I think anyone can provide to help someone deal with his or her spiritual journey in order to experience wholeness and wellness. Because we all have a basic understanding of what's involved with spiritual care—even though there can be some significant differences in what that means—this is consistent with those who claim: "I can provide spiritual care" (like social workers, nurses, technicians, church members, and so forth).

Yes, there is no doubt that most anyone can provide this basic kind of spiritual support. But because a BCC is a specialist in spiritual care, s/he will tend to understand better and will go deeper than this basic type of spiritual care.

Pastoral Care

Pastoral Care is a step up from this basic spiritual care. By definition, the word "pastoral" implies the giving of spiritual guidance by a clergy member of a faith group that holds to a specific religious worldview.

This pastoral level of care is often provided by someone who has had some theological education and pastoral experience and may be the faith leader for a particular faith group. This is a more in-depth type of spiritual support than the basic spiritual care because the person has a background in theological education and pastoral experience. It is usually provided by and for those who share similar beliefs and practices (such as the Rabbi for Jewish patients and the Priest for Roman Catholic patients and the Protestant Pastor for the Protestant patients).

Basically, I see Clergy—these pastoral caregivers—as *general practitioners* in the provision of pastoral care at the bedside. They certainly know a lot about caring for the spiritual needs of the hurting, but their bedside ministry is usually not a main part of their focused experience and expertise—they are not specialists.

By definition, a "specialist" is someone who is qualified by *advanced* training (in other words, it goes *beyond basic* theological education) **plus** certification by a specialty examining board to practice in a specific area of expertise—in this case healthcare chaplaincy. A specialist is someone who has special knowledge and strengths and skills needed for the specialty task of spiritual support at the bedside. I see BCCs as specialists (professional experts) in the spiritual-pastoral care they provide within the healthcare setting.

Chaplaincy Care

That brings us to *Chaplaincy Care*. This is the spiritual, emotional, religious, theological, pastoral, and ethical care provided by a Board Certified Chaplain (BCC). It is the specialized spiritual support provided by a specialist in healthcare chaplaincy.

These professional healthcare Chaplains not only have theological education and pastoral experience, but they also have received extensive and intensive specialized clinical pastoral education in chaplaincy care at the bedside. In addition, they have been peer reviewed for the competency of this chaplaincy care they provide. They also adhere to a code of ethics for the chaplaincy care they provide and they are endorsed by their faith group for this type of specialized ministry.

Again, as I've already said, chaplaincy care (as with a BCC) is a level of skilled care—expertise, proficiency, know-how—that no one else can provide.

Requirements for a BCC

So, what are the requirements for these specialists in chaplaincy care—these Board Certified Chaplains? One of the requirements is *theological education*. This means a Board Certified Chaplain must have at least a Masters degree from a school of theology—a seminary. That's at least 64 graduate level units of instruction for a Masters degree in a field related to pastoral care and theology, and a Master of Divinity degree is at least 96 units (though this number can vary slightly from one seminary to another).

Why is this theological education requirement important for the practice of spiritual support at the bedside? The sick and suffering often have spiritual distress. A theological education can help Chaplains better understand these spiritual issues from a biblical perspective so they can respond to the various religious ideas and practices and needs of the people they serve.

Another requirement is *ordination* and *endorsement*. Why is this important? Ordination is confirmation by a faith group that a Chaplain has a calling to ministry, a basic understanding of theological issues, and they will stand behind his or her character. Endorsement is recognition by a faith group that this Chaplain has a calling to chaplaincy and meets their standards of character and competence to serve as a Chaplain. It demonstrates that the Chaplain is not a "Lone Ranger" and is accountable to a faith group as a minister.

In addition to theological education, ordination and endorsement, a BCC is also required to have at least 4 units (1,600 hours) of *clinical pastoral education* (often referred to as CPE). It may be obvious, but why is this requirement important? This is the specialized training in a specialized setting that helps one become a specialist. It's where a Chaplain learns sensitivity to multi-cultural and multi-faith situations and respect for patients' spiritual or religious preferences. It's through this process that a Chaplain learns about and develops his/her role as a Chaplain. It's where a Chaplain gains practical understanding of the impact of illness on individuals and their caregivers. This is where a Chaplain gains first-hand knowledge of healthcare dynamics in a healthcare setting. It's where a Chaplain learns about accountability to and working with a healthcare team.

In order to be a BCC with HCMA, even after the 1,600 hours of clinical pastoral education, the person will need an additional 1,600 hours of clinical experience as an Intern Chaplain. Why is this important? This is where a Chaplain sharpens his or her pastoral care skills and demonstrates clinical competency (similar to that of a residency for a medical doctor).

At the end of the internship, there is a peer review of the Chaplain's competency as a professional Chaplain, which leads to certification. What is the importance of this activity? Someone can be putting in the hours but not be competent. Certification is a recognition that a person has measured up to a set of standards through a peer review process.

Finally, a BCC is required to be involved in continuing education throughout the year. Why is this important? Staying "sharp" means continuing to be aware of chaplaincy care issues and how best to meet spiritual needs. A professional Chaplain is always learning, ever growing, always sharpening his or her chaplaincy care tools.

Chaplaincy Training

Let's take a further look at the importance of clinical pastoral education for those who serve as Chaplains. Regulatory and accrediting bodies (such as The Joint Commission) require sensitive attention to the spiritual needs of patients with and without faith. Being clinically educated helps a Chaplain know how to be sensitive and respectful to people's different cultural and religious beliefs and practices and needs. Professional Chaplains are trained to respond appropriately to people who have various values and beliefs and different worldviews, providing a more holistic approach to healthcare.

Being a healthcare Chaplain is different than being a Pastor. Chaplains are often ministering to people who don't share our faith or worldview, who come from a different culture and have different ideas about illness and wellness. Chaplaincy training helps Chaplains come alongside these people with respect and sensitivity for those differences without imposing one's own views and faith on them.

Board Certified Chaplains are trained to be available to everyone, regardless of their faith tradition or lack of it. They reach across faith boundaries and do not proselytize. It's never appropriate for a Chaplain to force or impose his/her faith on someone else. That's spiritual abuse and unprofessional conduct. Spiritual support is about *their* spiritual needs, not *my* spiritual agenda, and clinical pastoral education helps a Chaplain become comfortable with that tension between theology and practice.

Clinical pastoral education trains Chaplains to understand and respond to a health crisis as they help clients and families with healing and recovery. They listen for the impact of a crisis on clients and families and often help facilitate an understanding of the crisis, which is often complicated by medical terminology. During a crisis, Chaplains often serve as the liaison between the medical team and the patient and family, as well as the liaison between the medical team and Clergy. Clinical pastoral education helps a Chaplain to understand medical terminology and the medical system and often where that all fits together with faith and practice and wellness.

When a patient or resident and their family are faced with serious illness, a BCC has been trained to understand and respond to the need to reduce pain and instill peace. Improving quality of life is all about spiritual well-being and a professional Chaplain has been equipped to provide quality support in these palliative care situations. Professional Chaplains understand the difference between care that is primarily focused on trying to cure and care that is mainly focused on giving comfort when a cure is not possible.

Professional Chaplains are trained to participate in healthcare ethics consultations, especially since spiritual and religious issues are almost always connected with medical ethics issues. Local Clergy are not usually adequately trained to deal with these medical ethics matters like a BCC. Clinical pastoral education helps a Chaplain to understand and deal with the dilemmas of medical ethics.

Professional Chaplains are also trained to take care of themselves. Being around morbidity and mortality on a regular basis is stressful. A BCC has learned how to avoid compassion fatigue and how to help others cope with stress in their lives (especially staff).

To summarize some of the benefits of clinical pastoral education:

- It helps Chaplains understand their identity, which improves their function—the ability to come alongside and comfort the hurting.
- It equips Chaplains to better understand their role in wellness—as primarily comforters rather than correctors.
- It improves the quality of care provided by Chaplains—which improves patient and resident wellness and satisfaction.
- It is good for business from the institution's perspective, and it's good for well-being from the patient's and resident's perspective—it's all about excellence and quality of care.

To learn more about clinical pastoral education, contact Healthcare Chaplains Ministry Association (HCMA) at (714) 572-3626 or info@hcmachaplains.org.

HCMA is the Healthcare Chaplains Ministry Association. Founded in 1939, HCMA is a non-sectarian, non-profit professional chaplaincy organization that recruits, trains, certifies and encourages Christian Chaplains serving in healthcare facilities (both acute, long term, and end-of-life care) worldwide. HCMA is clinically trained and professionally competent Christian Chaplains who provide spiritual counsel and emotional support to patients and residents, their family members, and healthcare staff, regardless of their worldview. HCMA Chaplains function as an integral member of the healthcare team to meet the spiritual and emotional needs of the sick and suffering, the downhearted and dying. Check out our website at www.hcmachaplains.org.

Endnotes

Preface

1. Unless otherwise noted, all Scripture references are from the *New King James Version* (Nashville: Thomas Nelson, 1982).
2. Katie Maxwell, *Bedside Manners: A Practical Guide to Visiting the Ill* (Grand Rapids, MI: Baker, 1990): 98.

Chapter 1: Biblical Foundation for Pastoral Care: Love and Compassion

1. The information in this chapter has been adapted from the Doctoral Project of Chaplain Peggy Jo Wobbema, BCC with HCMA, *The Development of an Integrated Pastoral Care Response System to Illness, Crisis, and Grief at North Point Church, Springfield, Missouri*. Copyright © Peggy Jo Wobbema, 2007. It is used with permission.
2. While focusing on God's love and compassion in this chapter, there is no intent to overlook or minimize God's other attributes of holiness, righteousness, and justice. Though gracious, God is also cognizant of sinfulness. One of His purposes is to cleanse and purify from sin. But even His discipline is carried out in love (Hebrews 12:6). As we seek to display God's love

and compassion to others, may we also balance this truth with His holiness and justice in mind.

3. Arthur F. Glasser and Charles Edward Van. Engen *Announcing the Kingdom: The Story of God's Mission in the Bible* (Grand Rapids, MI: Baker Academic, 2003): 52.

4. See Genesis 12:1-4; 13:14-17; 15:1-7, 18-21; and 17:1-8 for this covenant between God and Abraham.

5. Peggy Jo Wobbema, statement made during a seminar presentation on "The Biblical Foundation for Pastoral Care," Belleville, IL, September 16, 2006.

6. The consensus of Bible scholars seems to be that this Psalm was post-exilic (and we're not sure who the human author is), being written in the time when the remnant came back from Babylon to restore Hebrew national life in the promised land — and God's *hesed* was still with them (as it is with us)!

7. Kenneth S. Wuest, *Wuest's Word Studies from the Greek New Testament for the English Reader*, Volume III (Grand Rapids, MI: Wm. B. Eerdmans Pub., 1975): 110, 112.

8. Lawrence O. Richards, *Expository Dictionary of Bible Words* (Grand Rapids, MI: Zondervan, 1985): 180.

9. Ian Gentles, ed., *Care for the Dying and Bereaved* (Toronto: Anglican Book Centre, 1982): 49.

10. Henri J. M. Nouwen, *The Way of the Heart: Connecting with God through Prayer, Wisdom, and Silence* (New York: Ballantine, 2003): 33-34.

Chapter 2: Pastoral Care at the Bedside: Dos and Don'ts

1. Pastor Mike Slater calls them "Stretcher Bearers" in his book by the same name (Regal, 1985). I highly recommend that you read this very practical application of caring for others in need.

2. Wm. G. Justice, *Training Guide for Visiting the Sick* (New York: Haworth Pastoral, 2005): 18-19.

3. Ibid, 19.

4. One study of pre-op patients done many years ago showed that 75% of patients had some type of fear or anxiety before their surgery. From my own experience as a Chaplain I suspect that

the other 25% were probably not being open and vulnerable about their real feelings.

5. My personal definition of minor surgery is this: "Minor surgery is surgery done on someone else."

Chapter 3: Empathic Listening

1. I may not share all of Levine's worldview concerning other issues of life, but his comment about attentive presence is worth thinking about as we work on sharpening our listening skills as a pastoral caregiver.
2. Regardless of what you may think of Dr. Rogers' ideas about psychology, I think he got this view right and this statement should stimulate some reflective thinking about our own listening skills.
3. I may not endorse Thoreau's general philosophy of life, but this statement is thought provoking when it comes to good pastoral care listening skills.
4. Terry Felber, *Am I Making Myself Clear?: Secrets of the World's Greatest Communicators* (Nashville: Thomas Nelson, 2002): 53.
5. David Augsburger, *Caring Enough to Hear and be Heard* (Ventura, CA: Regal, 1982): 12, emphasis added.
6. Mary Pellauer in *God's Fierce Whimsy: Christian Feminism and Theological Education*, Mud Flower, ed. (Cleveland, OH: Pilgrim, 1985), emphasis added.
7. Henri J. M. Nouwen, *Care and the Elderly*, (New York: Ministers and Missionaries Benefit Board of the American Baptist Churches, 1975): 5, emphasis added.
8. Marie Riediger, "The Art of Listening to Hurting People," *Direction* Vol. 21, No. 1 (Spring 1992): 64-72.
9. Juanita R. Ryan, *Standing By* (Wheaton, IL: Tyndale House Pub., 1984): 89, emphasis added.
10. Ken Sharp, Rapha Christian Counseling Center, Irving, TX, emphasis added.
11. Organization Strategy Institute (OSI), under "The Awesome Power of the Listening Ear," at http://www.kenosi.com/aple (accessed July 2008).

12. The following is adapted from Juanita R. Ryan, *Standing By* (Wheaton, IL: Tyndale House Pub., 1984): 79-86.
13. Wayne E. Oates, *The Presence of God in Pastoral Counseling* (Waco, TX: Word, 1986): 70.
14. Ryan, *Standing By*, 90.

Chapter 4: Coming Alongside Patients and Residents

1. Michael A. Milton, "So What Are You Doing Here? The Role of the Minister of the Gospel in Hospital Visitation, or a Theological Cure for the Crisis in Evangelical Pastoral Care," *Journal of Evangelical Theological Society* 46, No. 3 (September 2003): 449-463. This article is worth reading in its entirety. A copy can be found at www.etsjets.org/files/JETS-PDFs/46/46-3/46-3-pp449-463_JETS.pdf.
2. Kenneth J. Doka, ed., with John D. Morgan, *Death and Spirituality* (Amityville, NY: Baywood Pub., 1993).
3. Lawrence E. Holst, ed., *Hospital Ministry: The Role of the Chaplain Today* (New York: Crossroad, 1985): 12.
4. Frederic Greeves, *Theology and the Cure of Souls* (Manhasset, NY: Channel, 1962), quoted by C. W. Brister in *Pastoral Care in the Church* (New York: Harper & Row, 1977): 66-67.
5. Carroll Wise, *A Clinical Approach to the Problems of Pastoral Care* (Boulder, CO: Western Interstate Commission for Higher Education, 1964): 87.
6. Milton, 454.
7. Ibid, 455-459.
8. Ralph G. Turnbull, "The Pastor as Comforter," in *Baker's Dictionary of Practical Theology*, Ralph G. Turnbull, ed. (Grand Rapids, MI: Baker, 1967), 299-300.
9. Milton, 455.
10. Ibid.
11. The HCMA Clinical Pastoral Education program includes a manual on Medical Terminology to encourage Chaplains to better understand the language being used around them. However, learning the information in the medical manual does not make us a medical expert nor is it the focus of our role as

Chaplains, nor should it be the main focus of any pastoral caregiver.

12. Milton, 455.
13. Ibid, 457.
14. Katie Maxwell, *Bedside Manners: A Practical Guide to Visiting the Ill* (Grand Rapids, MI: Baker, 1990): 31.
15. Milton, 458.
16. Patrick Fairbairn, *Pastoral Theology: A Treatise on the Office and Duties of the Christian Pastor* (Audubon, NJ: Old Paths, 1992 ed. of the 1875 orig. printed by T & T Clark, Edinburgh): 301.
17. Ibid.
18. For some, the laying on of hands may include the practice of *Reiki.* The word comes from two Japanese words: *rei* (meaning universal, spiritual consciousness, or higher intelligence) and *ki* (life energy). This New Age practice is sometimes referred to as "energy healing." Most who practice it do not credit God as the source of healing, but the *ki.* It has Buddhist roots and it encourages putting trust in ourselves and in *ki*, rather than God. *Reiki* should not be practiced by Christians.
19. This is the title frequently used for the Bible by Dr. Robert L. Reymond, a theologian of the Protestant Reformed tradition, best known for his *A New Systematic Theology of the Christian Faith* (Thomas T. Nelson, 1998).
20. R. Laird Harris, ed. *Theological Wordbook of the Old Testament* (Chicago, IL: Moody, 1980): 1:296.
21. Lawrence O. Richards, *Expository Dictionary of Bible Words* (Grand Rapids: MI, Zondervan, 1985): 180.
22. Ibid, 440.
23. Henri J.M. Nouwen, *Out of Solitude: Three Meditations on the Christian Life* (Notre Dame, IN: Ave Maria, 2004).
24. Neville A. Kirkwood, *Pastoral Care in Hospitals* (Harrisburg, PA: Moorehouse Pub., 1998):115.

Chapter 5: Coming Alongside the Dying

1. Jim Towns, *A Family Guide to Death and Dying* (Wheaton, IL: Tyndale House Pub., 1987): 133.

2. Much of this information is adapted from *Ministering to the Dying*, by Carl J. Scherzer (Prentice-Hall, 1963): 369-376; and from a booklet written by Jeffrey Funk, *As Someone Dies—What to Expect?* (FHRMC, 1994).

3. This five-stage grief reaction is outlined in detail by Elisabeth Kübler-Ross in her classic book: *On Death and Dying* (New York: Scribner Classics, 1997).

4. Joyce Landorf Heatherley, *Mourning Song*, revised-expanded ed. (Grand Rapids, MI: F. H. Revell, 1994): 53.

5. Joseph Bayly, *The View from a Hearse*, revised and expanded ed. (Elgin, IL: David C. Cook, 1973).

6. Heatherley, *Mourning Song*, 83-84.

7. E. Mansell Pattison, *Experience of Dying* (Upper Saddle River, NJ: Prentice-Hall, 1977). Dr. Pattison was the Deputy Director of Training, Consultation and Education Division of the Orange County Department of Mental Health, and was the Chairman of the Department of Psychiatry at the University of California, Irvine.

8. See Kenneth J. Doka, *Counseling Individuals with Life-Threatening Illness* (New York: Springer, 2009).

9. Adapted from Barney G. Glaser and Anselm L. Strauss, *Awareness of Dying* (Chicago: Aldine, 1965).

10. Therese A. Rando, ed., *Loss and Anticipatory Grief*, (Lanham, MD: Lexington, 1986).

Chapter 6: Coming Alongside Grieving People

1. The previous chapter on "Coming Alongside the Dying" already dealt with the fears of the dying, the dying stages, and more specifics on how to minister to them. Refer back to this chapter if you need to review this information.

2. This graph (Figure 2) on the shock and numbness that follows the death of a loved one comes from Glen W. Davidson, *Understanding Mourning* (Minneapolis, MN: Augsburg, 1984): 59. He also has a graph for disorientation and searching/yearning that equally shows the long-term (two-year average) ups and downs (waves) of adjusting to a significant loss.

3. The following is adapted from J. William Worden, *Grief Counseling and Grief Therapy: A Handbook for the Mental Health Practitioner* (New York: Springer, 1982). For a deeper understanding of these tasks, read this excellent resource on the subject.
4. Adapted from Bob Deits, *Life After Loss: A Personal Guide Dealing with Death, Divorce, Job Change and Relocation* (Tucson, AZ: Fisher, 1992): 61-74. This excellent resource also includes guidelines for forming a grief support group.
5. Adapted from Alan D. Wolfelt, *Death and Grief: A Guide for Clergy* (New York: Brunner-Rutledge, 1988): 115-119. Used with permission.

Chapter 7: Handling Emergencies

1. I may not agree with Sullivan's overall worldview, but this statement is worth thinking about as we consider how to respond to hurting people in an emergency situation.
2. Also see the chapters on "Empathic Listening" and "Coming Alongside Patients and Residents."
3. Chaplain Thomas E. Webb, Board Member of the National Center for Chaplain Development (NCCD) and International Faculty Member of International Critical Incident Stress Foundation (ICISF), developed these "yardsticks" from course material from the International Critical Incident Stress Foundation for assessing the severity of a critical incident and the impact of the emanating shock wave upon a person. Used with permission.
4. Pastoral caregivers can gain advanced training in critical incident stress management through the National Center for Chaplain Development (NCCD; www.nccdat.org).
5. *Manual on Hospital Chaplaincy*, American Hospital Association (1970):11.

Chapter 8: Boundaries for Effective Ministry

1. I may not agree with Flaubert's overall philosophy of life, but this statement is certainly thought provoking when it comes to thinking about boundaries in ministry.
2. Archibald D. Hart, "Walking on the Edge: The Counselor's Sexuality," *Christian Counseling Today* 7, No. 3 (1999): 20.
3. Mark R. Laaser, "Therapists Who Offend," *Christian Counseling Today* 6, No. 1 (1998): 59.
4. Anne Katherine, *Where to Draw the Line* (New York: Simon & Schuster, 2000).
5. From a personal conversation with Ken Royer.
6. Thomas A. Fischer, "7 Things Every Counselor Should Know to Nurture Congregational Health," *Christian Counseling Today* 10, No. 3 (2002): 23-24.
7. This subject is covered quite well by Kenneth Haugk, founder of Stephen Ministries, in Chapter 9 of *Christian Caregiving: A Way of Life* (Minneapolis, MN: Augsburg, 1984), 71-80. I urge you to read the whole book.
8. Personal advice from Ken Royer, pastoral counselor with Link Care Center in Fresno, CA.
9. Anne Underwood, "Toxic Humor," *PlainViews* 4, No. 7 (May 2, 2007).
10. Read chapter on "Avoiding Compassion Fatigue: Balancing the Burdens of Caregiving" for a full discussion about self-care.
11. Henry Cloud and John Townsend, *Boundaries in Marriage* (Grand Rapids, MI: Zondervan, 1999): 59.
12. Gary L. Harbaugh, Rebecca Lee Brenneis and Rodney R. Hutton, *Covenants & Care: Boundaries in Life, Faith, and Ministry* (Minneapolis, MN: Fortress, 1998): 17.

Chapter 9: Avoiding Compassion Fatigue: Balancing the Burdens of Caregiving

1. I may not share Keen's overall worldview, but his comment about burnout is worth thinking about as we get involved in pastoral care.

2. Herbert J. Freudenberger and Geraldine Richelson, *Burnout: The High Cost of High Achievement* (Garden City, New York: Doubleday, 1980): 16.
3. Christina Maslach, *Burnout: The Cost of Caring* (New York: Prentice-Hall, 1982): 3.
4. Herbert Freudenberger and Geraldine Richelson, *Burn-Out* (New York: Doubleday, 1980): 62-66.
5. Herbert J. Freudenberger and Geraldine Richelson, *Burnout: The High Cost of High Achievement* (Toronto: Bantam, 1981).
6. Studies show that most adults need at least eight hours per night but only get about six!
7. Frederic Flach, *Resilience: Discovering a New Strength at Times of Stress*, Revised ed. (New York: Hatherleigh, 2003).
8. If you need some help in getting started, I recommend reading *The Rewarding Practice of Journal Writing: A Guide for Starting and Keeping Your Personal Journal* by James E. Miller (Fort Wayne, IN: Willowgreen, 1998).
9. David A Ruch, "Final Word: The Hidden Healings," *Christian Counseling Today* 5, No. 3 (1997): 70.
10. The 8th century words of "Art Thou Weary, Art Thou Languid?" were originally written in Greek by Stephen of Mar Saba. It was translated into English by John M. Neale in 1862 and the music was composed by Henry W. Baker in 1868.
11. Rick Warren, *Piers Morgan Live*, aired on CNN September 17, 2013.